FINANCIAL
TROUBLESHOOTING

FINANCIAL TROUBLESHOOTING

An Action Plan for Money Management in the Small Business

David H. Bangs , Jr.
and
The Editors of *Common Sense*

Upstart Publishing Company, Inc.
The Small Business Publishing Company
Dover, New Hampshire

Published by Upstart Publishing Company, Inc.
A Division of Dearborn Publishing Group, Inc.
12 Portland Street
Dover, New Hampshire 03820
(800) 235-8866 or (603) 749-5071

Neither the author nor the publisher of this book is engaged in rendering, by the sale of this book, legal, accounting or other professional services. The reader is encouraged to employ the services of a competent professional in such matters.

Library of Congress Cataloging-in-Publication Data

Bangs, David H.
    Financial troubleshooting: an action plan for money management in the
        small business [edited by] David H. Bangs, Jr. and the editors of Common
        sense.
        p.   cm.
    Includes index.
    ISBN 0-936894-37-7
    1. Small business--Finance. I. Bangs, David H. II.Common sense
(Portsmouth, N.H.)
    HG4027.7.F555   1992
    658.15'92--dc20   92-30261
                                                                            CIP

Cover design by Pear Graphic Design, Portsmouth, NH.

Printed in the United States of America
10 9 8 7 6 5 4 3 2

For a complete catalog of Upstart's small business publications, call (800) 235-8866.

Table
of Contents

....

Foreword

....

Financial Troubleshooting is a compilation of financial management articles originally published in *Common Sense Management Techniques*.

Common Sense is a newsletter that Upstart syndicates to clients ranging in size from small local banks to the very largest banks in the U.S. These banks share an interest in helping their small business customers become more profitable and stronger, figuring that those small businesses that grew would be receptive to more sophisticated services than equipment loans and commercial checking accounts. Those businesses that remained small would continue out to be highly profitable to the banks—loyal customers who in a major bank study were shown to be valuable providers of funds to the banks.

In our conversations with bankers throughout the country during *Common Sense*'s fifteen year's, several points kept recurring:

1.   Simple things work best. Complexity flops.

2.   Positive cash flow equals survival.

3.   Forecasting and planning characterize profitable businesses, pleases bankers, and provides the foundation for strong growth.

4.   Businesses which use tight, carefully thought out budgets succeed. If they stumble, they can be picked up, dusted off, and sent forward—but businesses without budgets collapse without a chance to redeem themselves.

5.   Small business owners don't like to spend a lot of time with numbers. A surprising number strangle their potential by being "too busy to keep records." Another large group shoots themselves in the foot by proudly proclaiming they don't "waste money on an accountant." Then they get angry when bankers ask for information before granting a loan.

We do our best to be mindful of the needs of the small business owners who are the banks' customers. Upstart has the advantage of seeing both sides of the bank/customer relationship. We work with and talk with bankers and small business owners—and can identify with the problems on either side. As a small business owner myself I made most of the financial mistakes that can be made and somehow survived them, but at the cost of a lot of wasted time and squandered effort. As a former banker I had already seen most of these, which might lead you to wonder why I didn't avoid them. I have no idea.

Prevention is the best cure for financial problems. Setting up information flows so that problems are spotted early on is common sense. So is looking carefully ahead, setting and following budgets, and making sure that growth doesn't outstrip cash flows. The *Common Sense* articles reflect these notions.

The chapters in this book provide a series of steps for you to follow, frequently using forms and checklists to make your job easier. We recommend using outside advisors in technical areas. For example, the complex and frustrating matter of following and applying over 35,000 pages of tax code without getting squashed or penalized is best left to your accountant.

Your thinking and experience are important in all aspects of your business. You have to help the accountant or consultant set up your information flow. You have to make decisions about what is important to follow closely, what can be ignored or left until later. You have to decide what constitutes adequate sales and profits for your business—and budget accordingly. You have to monitor your company's progress by comparing actual performance to projected or budgeted performance. This doesn't mean you have to turn into a bean counter. Far from it. You have a business to run and these financial measures are very helpful to you. They are designed to help you spot problems and opportunities and make more money.

You do have to be able to use the information that your financial systems provide as readily as you use other forms of information. If some piece of information puzzles you or doesn't make sense, ask for help. Your banker, accountant, bookkeeping service, financial consultant or Small Business Development Center counselor can help you. The net result is that you will make better decisions faster than you would otherwise. You'll spend less time financial troubleshooting and more time making money.

—David H. "Andy" Bangs, Jr., editor
Portsmouth, New Hampshire

Chapter One:

Organizing Information Needs

....

W e live in an era of rapid change. At one time it may have been possible to run a solid business on hunch and habit, because the rate of change was slow enough to enable a company, once set on the right path, to continue down that path with little danger. Not any more.

Every business generates a stream of information. The prosperous business, the carefully managed growing business, uses that information as an integral part of the managerial strategy.

Decisions come in three modes: hunch-based, habit-based and information-based. Our bias is for the last of these, since it can include the first two while testing them on an ongoing basis. Hunches are fine: They provide insights into your business, encourage you to enter new markets in spite of apparent obstacles, and perform an energizing function. However, for every hunch that does succeed, many do not. The hunch monitored by information gains you the best of both worlds. Your hunch is a reflection of your experience and intelligence, and the information is a backup.

Habits are also fine. They save time and free us up to do more than we could do otherwise. But if we don't occasionally step back and check to be sure that our habits are useful, we may find that they have become counterproductive.

Rather than risk disaster (assuming that these are major decisions), you want to make sure that you have a reasonable information base to test your hunches and habits before charging ahead. Over time, your decisions will be only as good as the information you base them on.

Ensuring a clear, consistent and coherent information flow is not an easy task. You need to rely on your accountant's skills. You may have to call in a consultant to set your information system up—you know what information would be desirable to have in many instances, and what timing is needed. But all of us get so close to our own businesses that we have trouble seeing the forest for the trees. That's where the outside experts can be invaluable.

Your information needs will vary. As a general rule, considerations of cost of information, timeliness, level of detail and applicability are the most important. And your time is valuable. So you need organized, concise information that sums up the activities of your company in a useful way.

The six steps of organizing your information needs will help you get what you need, when you need it—at a price and level of detail that makes sense for your company.

Outline the Ten Most Important Decisions

The first step in establishing the right information flow for your business is to take a close look at the important decisions that your business faces in the near future. As a practical exercise, this has several benefits.

First, it's an excellent planning tool. All of us have a number of decisions we are expected to make, some of which are more important than others. Yet if you're anything like the rest of us, you seldom take time to rank the decisions in terms of potential impact, importance and long-term effects.

Second, as you list the ten most important decisions you face, you will probably find that the first five or six are obvious. The remainder take a bit more thought.

Check over your completed list, and ask yourself the following questions:

Can I make a decision on the information I have available? Would more information help?

Ideally, what kind of information would I use to make these decisions?

Can I get that information? How? When? At what cost?

What is the minimum amount of information I would feel comfortable with?

We suggest you then rank the decisions in terms of long-range impact, since this will help focus your attention on the more important problems.

Ask yourself: What major decision have I been putting off? Why?

Most of us know that there are decisions that for one reason or another we are avoiding. These can include financial decisions (Can we afford to expand?), strategic decisions (Should we open a branch office?) and/or emotionally painful decisions (Should I fire Harvey?) In all major decisions well organized information will make a positive difference.

Your list need not be exhaustive or perfect. The purpose of the list (and of the questions the list will raise) is to find a starting point for establishing the proper information flow for your company, based on your knowledge of its operations and goals. Refining the list can come later. For now, the list alone will be helpful.

List Activities to Monitor

What activities go on in your business? The challenge is to see how these activities fit together—and what they involve that doesn't show up at first glance.

Examples of the kinds of activities you want to control are (1) cash flow, (2) sales/marketing activities, and (3) production.

Cash flow is pretty straightforward: If you spend more than you take in, sooner or later the negative cash flow kills the business—while if you consistently take in more than you spend, the positive cash flow will let you pay dividends. Look at item five in Figure 1.1.

Case in Point: ABC Manufacturing

"A new product we're considering will cause a severe cash drain (no project we undertake shows an instant positive cash flow), so at the very minimum, we have to know how much of a drain we will face. We also need to know what we have coming in and going out on a normal basis; we don't want to start a new line that we can't afford. Ideally, we'd have a crystal clear view of the future cash flow—but that isn't possible. Although our present information system (a cash flow budget and the deviation analysis we measure ourselves by) provides adequate information, we need more timely information than we are getting, especially with a new project. Our aim is to have a separate cash flow for the new project, to allow us to be sure it doesn't cost us too heavily.

"Sales/marketing activities pose a different kind of problem. While they have a decided effect on cash flow, and are in a sense controlled by it, they really center on people. We have to know, for example, how well our direct mail campaign works, how many calls the sales force is making (and to whom), and how those calls translate into sales. Once that information is gained, personnel decisions can be made, marketing strategies can be evaluated, and added control over the marketing/sales activities is possible.

"Production problems and decisions are fairly clear. From purchasing raw materials to production of finished product (including quality control concerns), production is a linear process. The costs and the timing are not hidden—although the assembly process can become unwieldy. We need a handle on who can do what, how much lead time is needed, and how overburdened our work force is. We need to know what we'll be producing and in what quantities. For more sophisticated production problems, a far more detailed analysis would be needed.

"The main point is that the activities we want information about can be monitored in various ways. We try to pick the most adequate for us—in this case, tracking cash flow from a new product, keeping tabs on new sales personnel, and making as sure as we can that the new product moves ahead on schedule. We could define these further, but why bother? Managing a business requires some discrimination—enough detail to manage, not enough to render action impossible."

—Mr. A., President, ABC Manufacturing

Collect Accurate Data

Raw data is generated by any attempt to record what happens in a business. Usually, activities are measured in terms of money, units or time. Cash flow is measured in dollars and time; the idea is to learn how cash in motion operates. To keep tabs on new sales personnel, you need call reports and sales information. The orders are a further source of raw data, letting you know what is selling, and to whom.

This step almost always demands professional advice. The generation and ordering of raw data is where your accountant earns a lot of praise or blame. The chart of accounts he or she sets up to reflect your business activities will have far-reaching implications for your final information flow. If your chart of accounts is not done well, it can be worse than useless. You don't want to get stuck with a chart of accounts that doesn't reflect your business and your goals. This can be the result of using a prepackaged chart of accounts that fits the accountant's software at the expense of your business' information needs—so be careful to discuss the chart of accounts in detail with your accountant. Remember: You're the boss.

Hiring a first-rate accountant is an excellent investment. See Chapter Two: All About Accountants for ideas on how to locate the right one for your business.

Organize the Data

Raw data need considerable shaping before you can use them. As the information is generated, it needs to be summarized. For most businesses, this requires standard financial statements: balance sheets, profit and loss statements, cash flow analyses and budgets, and perhaps deviation analyses for the financial controls.

Most of us are familiar with these statements, though sometimes we forget that they are meant to be used to show how our business is performing. We're often guilty of the error of putting the financials aside "until we have time for them."

Learning about a problem or an opportunity too late is no way to run a business. One of the criteria for measuring the adequacy of our performance is to see how quickly we can identify and capitalize on new opportunities—and how quickly we can solve problems.

For sales/marketing control, you need a way of summarizing the salesperson's performance on either a monthly or weekly basis, as seems indicated. Ask for a summary of calls made and orders placed, and a report on customer suggestions, criticisms and other ideas.

For any personnel decisions, some basic information is mandatory. To evaluate the people fairly, document what they do. What about attendance? Ever try to fire someone for poor attendance and then not be able to provide the dates involved? The data needed may be exceptions: "Absent for 18 consecutive Fridays

Figure 1.1

Start with a List of Decisions

At ABC Manufacturing, the final list came out as follows:

1. New product decision;

2. Personnel: new production foreman, some marketing and administrative persons;

3. Work flow: internal operations planning;

4. Relocation;

5. Cash flow problem: enlarge budget;

6. Do a marketing survey;

7. Shareholder agreement for new company;

8. New equipment;

9. Use more part-time staff or hire full-time help;

10. Clarify chain of command.

Note that this is general. It covers many areas and names the broader problem in these areas without going into detail.

. . . ." The summary form should cover those aspects of performance which are most important, otherwise it won't be useful or used.

Use the Data

The final step is interpreting the data and putting it to work.

Cash flow reports, for example, are not informative by themselves. They must be compared to some standard—that is, interpreted—before they become informative.

That's your job. The initial data-gathering and compilation can (and in most cases should) be delegated. Using the data is a different matter. This task cannot be safely or lightly given to someone else.

The financial and other summaries contain a huge amount of information to help you manage your business. Your accountant or your bookkeeper can't apply the information, and they can't use it to manage your business.

> **Figure 1.2**
>
> **The Keys to Using Data**
>
> 1. Measure activities selectively.
>
> 2. Compile pieces of information into reports (summaries, aggregates).
>
> 3. Make sure these are timely and understandable by the owner/manager, not just by the accountant or experts.
>
> 4. Compare summaries with standards; take action where needed.

Your time is limited. As the owner/manager, you can only look at the summaries—the tip of the iceberg, so to speak. If they show some deviation (worse or better than usual), you might then have to get into the details. Otherwise, leave them alone. You have enough to do as it is.

Look for deviations first, trends second. If the cash flow gets sticky, monitor the details—daily, in some cases, rather than monthly or quarterly. If sales are slow, pay the same attention to daily sales reports. If production is stalled for some reason, give it immediate attention—no product means no sales, no cash flow.

But remember: If you don't have standards by which to measure projected cash flow, actual balance between receivables and payables, sales quotas, historical sales data, a measure for relating the number of calls to sales, some product completion dates and quality standards, all the data in the world won't do you any good.

Implement Information Flow; Review Regularly

As a managerial strategy, using information flow as outlined in the preceding steps is a version of management by exception. You set the standards—based on your knowledge and experience. Your business plan probably states many of them clearly—sales per month; cash flow and budgeting figures; personnel policies on vacations, days off and sick pay, to name a few. When an exception occurs, you want to know why.

Make your information flow system a managerial priority item to be reviewed carefully at least annually, review and adjust your strategy whenever there is a major change in your business.

How much time does it take to implement a careful information flow strategy? Less than you might think, since a large part of it can and probably should be performed by outside advisors. You may not want to hire a consultant—but consider the following sources of help:

- trade journals
- your accountant
- your banker
- the Small Business Administration's SCORE, SBDC and SBI programs

- textbooks
- other publications, such as SBA material (or better yet, Upstart's books)

How do you formulate an information strategy? Return to the very first step. What are the ten most important decisions you have to make during the next year?

By now, you can ask what summary information would help make those decisions better—and work backward. For example, you need to have financial statements, including balance sheets, profit and loss statements, cash flow reports and budgets, to make good cash flow decisions. These statements will depend on accurate sales and cost figures, which will also be generating another set of questions such as, "Are we getting the right/reasonable amount of return from our most profitable customers? What are they telling us? Are there other products we can develop for them? For allied markets?"

Try running this process both forward and backward. Begin with the most important activities and go forward; look at the most important decisions and go backward.

Why? Because the aim of establishing a clear, legitimate information flow is to manage the activities of your business better. The information and the activities affect each other, and your job is to see that that set of interrelations is making your job easier, more profitable.

Once again: What decisions are you facing? What information would make those decisions easier or better? Can you get that information? If not, what can you do to get that information (within the bounds of cost and time)?

Use your information flow. It makes your hunches better, helps you see which habits are good and which are harmful, and will prove itself on your bottom line.

Summary

Information is only useful if you use it—and if it is accurate.

When assessing your information needs, keep timeliness and cost in view. Too many reports will get you bogged down; too few and you will run unnecessary risks.

Your aim is to manage by exception: The reports (organized data) should be compared to standards and action taken only when there is a reason to take action. Look into deviations only when they are sizable enough to warrant your attention.

Figure 1.3

Examples of Information Flow

Identify Activities

purchasing	stocking	collecting
paying	organizing	producing
marketing	borrowing	planning
scheduling	controlling	hiring
selling		

Measure Raw Data

sales	cost of selling
overhead	cost of materials
units of product produced	timing
employee attendance	employee performance

Organize Data

balance sheet	attendance
production reports	income statement sales reports
ratios	acid test
trends	

Compare With Standards

historical	industrial	projections
experience	insight	

Analyze Results of Comparison (New Information)

liquidity is low, leverage high
receivables high and old, payables okay
sales low, profits low
employee turn over high
secretary frequently late and absent

Make Decisions

improve collection procedure
identify strong and weak sales personnel
control extravagant selling costs
improve marketing
purchase and stock in economic units

Implement New Activities

Action Plan For:
Organizing Information Needs

☐ Outline and prioritize the ten most important decisions you have to make, including the painful ones you are avoiding.

☐ List the business activities you want to monitor.

☐ Collect accurate data.

☐ Organize the data in standard forms (such as financial statements, call reports, order lists).

☐ Use the data. Schedule time to review the information regularly.

☐ Implement information flow; review it periodically.

Chapter Two:

All About Accountants

....

In Chapter One: Organizing Information Needs accountants were referred to several times. Your choice of an accountant is extremely important. The right consultant will more than pay for him—or herself; the wrong one can cost you serious dollars. Or—worse—fail to give you the kind of information you need to remain competitive.

Introduction

They're the folks some of us love to hate: the faceless number crunchers whose only goal seems to be telling us how much money we don't have and how much money we can't spend.

All myths aside, accountants are more valuable than ever before, offering a whole host of new services aimed directly at the small business owner.

But finding the one that's exactly right for you can be like searching for the proverbial needle in the haystack—particularly if you've put your hunting off until tax time.

There are some things you can do—and know—to make your mission much easier, for you and your accountant.

Knowledge of the profession, skillful preparation, proper selection procedures and good communication—plus some chemistry—will help ease the search.

Keeping Track of Money in the Old Days

Accountants, shirt sleeves pushed high with green visors to shield their eyes, were considered slaves of sums. Perfect penmanship was a matter of pride. Caution, not client contact, was valued.

The profession's roots are in early history. The first accounts were recorded in stone, scratched in moist clay, then baked or hardened for posterity's sake.

More careful accounting was necessary in Great Britain during the 1100's. High finance was reserved for royalty, though. Counters representing pence and pounds were placed within lines chalked on a cloth covered table. Sums were recorded in a narrative form.

In the 1300's, figures were moved to the right-hand side of a page. Later, Arabic numbers replaced Roman numerals, though pages of accounts could be grandly illuminated or illustrated.

After all, a businesses venturing a single service or product, long before computers and credit cards, hardly had a need for complicated analysis of what was earned and what was spent.

Even Dr. Johnson sided with simplicity: "Keeping accounts, Sir, is of no use when a man is spending his own money and has nobody to whom he is to account You won't eat less beef today because you have written down what it cost yesterday."

But the days of keeping sums with counters on a colored tablecloth are over. Accounting is a regulated profession requiring specialized training and measured against high standards set by the profession and government agencies.

The Evolution of the Species

In the United States, the profession dates back to the 1800's when the first professional organization meeting drew barely 30 people. The group thereafter lobbied for and won licensing in the state of New York in 1896.

Now, every state certifies public accountants. The U.S. Department of Labor estimates some 900,000 accountants, about a third of them certified, are at work across the country.

Certification is rigorous, and would-be CPAs must first earn a bachelor's degree. The new graduate must then sit for the Uniform CPA exam. The grueling two and a half-day exam, prepared and graded by the American Institute of Certified Public Accountants, covers theory and practice of auditing and accounting. The test is given twice a year in the 50 states, the District of Columbia, Puerto Rico, the Virgin Islands and Guam.

Individual state boards of accountancy then grant the CPA certification. They also issue licenses to practice required of CPAs who practice publicly on their own or in accounting firms. The license is not required of CPAs who work in education, government or private industry.

In a majority of states, CPAs who practice publicly must also complete 40 hours of continuing professional education—known in CPA shorthand as CPEs—every year. The CPEs may come through conferences, seminars or special courses.

Some states also require CPAs to meet an experience requirement For example, in Michigan, a CPA must earn a BA with a concentration in accounting, pass the uniform exam and have two years of public accounting experience.

Degree, exam and experience accounted for, the new CPA typically seeks work. Accounting firms generally recruit on campus, seeking the cream of the campus crop. Some create internships, then hire from that pool. Many hire new MBAs.

Results reported in a recent national survey of accountants and their jobs notes that:

About 50 percent of the nation's CPAs work in local accounting firms.

CPAs tend to work as generalists, performing a wide variety of tasks, though the work depends on the nature of their clients or the firm that employs them.

The average CPA is young, not quite 40 years old. Younger CPAs are more likely to be found in large firms. Veterans tend to work in local firms or in sole practices.

The majority of CPAs have undergraduate college degrees.

Senior level staff members, partners and accountants in solo practices were more likely to handle consulting tasks than were staff members with less experience.

Changing times have called for large and small firms alike to reconsider traditions.

Though CPAs' tasks may differ slightly, their main duties are to provide services to clients. Historically, large firms concentrated their services with larger businesses and small accounting firms focused their services on small business. By custom and tradition, businesses rarely changed accountants.

But changing times have called for large and small firms alike to reconsider traditions in light of recent work place trends.

Decentralized work groups, younger and better educated workers, more women in the work force, a high-tech, high-touch society that does away with routine jobs and eliminates employment for the unskilled laborers have accountants' attention.

The recognition is coming that a small business one week may grow dramatically the next, and that electronic cottages and new-wave workers are demanding new kinds of specialized financial help that call for CPAs to be known as more than pencil pushers.

Trend-watching accountants—armed with computers and super-calculators—are starting to offer clients a virtual smorgasbord of financial, management and consulting services.

These specialized, and to some extent, customized services are marketed, targeted or sold under names like expanded services or management advisory services—MAS in accounting shorthand.

They may also include such once-exotic things as newsletters, software design and installation, teams set up especially to solve small business problems, financial planning seminars for spouses or training sessions on tax and financial topics.

Knowing When to Get Help

"Stable businesses providing unchanging products to customers with unswerving loyalties may not need accounting services beyond basic bookkeeping," notes Irving L. Blackman, a frequently published CPA and partner in a Chicago accounting firm.

But almost every other small business may, at one time or another, need to employ an outside accountant or find inhouse help, temporary or permanent, he believes.

"Income isn't a measure," Blackman notes.

Other signals are: when your company confronts growth, economic or technological change, unfamiliar markets, new laws, tax complications, the need for a bank loan or outside financing, or a more demanding or dynamic environment.

Making the Perfect Match

Under such conditions, marrying the right accountant to your business is crucial and the selection decision becomes key. Take these steps as you look for a partner for your financial future:

1. Know your needs first. The first step is always the hardest, and assessing your need for simple or sophisticated financial services before you shop can be a complicated task.

Start by knowing where your business is . . . and then ask where you'd like it to be within the next week, the following month, next year, next five or ten years.

Compile a list of problems you'd like solved, improvements you'd like made, equipment you need to purchase, profits you'd like to generate.

A skilled accountant can ask questions that will draw out problems—and perhaps potential solutions—from you. "A skillful accountant will really find out . . . what you've got in your head," says CPA, Blackman.

Try to establish where problems exist, and how a CPA can help. Says Sam Hoyt director of media relations for the 240,000-member American Institute of CPAs: "The more you know beforehand, the better off you'll be."

2. Consult with friends, colleagues or business associates for CPAs they can recommend. "The best way to find a CPA is through references from friends or business associates who use one and are pleased with one," suggests Varley Simons, vice president of the Chicago-based American Society of Women CPAs and a partner in the Atlanta accounting firm of Gorbandt and Simons, PC.

Seek out leads from other business owners in your industry or from associations representing your trade or profession. Check with your banker, lawyer or state CPA society.

Some business publications issue their own directories of accountants and other financial professionals. Directories, for example, are published in Detroit, Houston, New England, New York and south Florida.

3. Compare the advantages—and disadvantages—of a large firm with a national reputation and a small firm with a local following. Contrast their services with your needs. "Don't necessarily be influenced by someone who tells you big is best," says Hoyt.

Look for a firm which is familiar with—or can learn quickly—the kind of work you need done.

4. Set up a personal interview. Ask in advance if fees are charged for the first consultation. Some CPAs levy charges; others may not, or may waive fees if you retain them.

Use the interview to ask questions and gather information you most need to know. Ask about education, professional experience and personal qualifications that pertain to your needs. Study qualifications before the interview, if possible, then structure the interview around questions about them.

Some considerations: study at an accredited institution, experience in methods and procedures, management consulting, contact with executives or experience developing, implementing and installing specialized programs.

You may also want to evaluate evidence of personal initiative, verbal and written communication skills, ability to obtain and analyze facts, diligence and use of imagination in solving small business problems.

Before the interview, devise a method for capturing information key to your final decision. A simple rating system may be helpful. You may want to include space for summary comments and any conclusions you've reached.

Allow sufficient time to complete your questioning, and convey interest and consideration for experienced professionals. Be courteous: Don't burn bridges in communicating your final decision.

5. Ask for references. "They should be checked too," advises Blackman. References don't always help you make the right match. "But it might help you not pick the wrong one," he says.

6. When you make your final selection, ask for an engagement letter. Most CPAs now charge by the hour, and any accountant should provide you with the letter, spelling out duties and fees.

Services provided by a senior-level partner may be more costly than those provided by a staff member. Those requiring frequent, detailed or customized reports may be more costly than routine statements at widely spaced intervals. CPAs in major cities may be more expensive than those in rural areas.

Key Questions

The worst way to find a CPA is to "call one up and hire him," sight unseen, Blackman believes.

He recommends that every candidate be asked the same questions. Among his dozen key questions to ask:

Is timely service delivered?

Will the same people always service your account?

What services beyond the usual reporting and number-crunching are offered?

How can you help me make money?

How are fees structured and calculated?

CPAs are urged to maintain good client relations, extend prompt service, take a sincere interest in clients, avoid arguments, return phone calls promptly and to treat clients as equals.

Chemistry

Despite your best efforts to evaluate a CPAs technical skills and ability, chemistry can count in the end, unless particular expertise is sought or the job to be done is simple. A CPA will ultimately become intimately familiar with your firm's finances—in sickness and in health. "You're going to want somebody you can work with," notes the AICPA's Hoyt.

"As the world turns, more small businesses are likely to turn to accountants for management that fits broadly into a financial framework," says California futurist Hank E. Koehn.

A CPA will ultimately become intimately familiar with your firm's finances —in sickness and in health.

"The action is in consulting services," says Koehn, president of the Los Angeles-based Trimtab Consulting Group. "Because of the trust that binds a business owner-operator to an accountant, the financial professional is in a unique position to offer advice on a variety of management issues," Koehn observes.

He forecasts that accountants will try to establish more personal relationships with clients, make new attempts to offer creative solutions to small business problems and more aggressively extend services to small businesses.

Accountants may have a greater role in small business decision-making, perhaps helping to identify, package and price services or recommend and install computer systems or software. Their financial planning services may increase. More may become specialists where specific industry needs can be targeted.

Because there are realistically a limited number of "billable" hours, fees may become more flexible, with some "unbundled" or specially packaged, Koehn predicts.

Whatever the future for the accounting industry in general, there are times when an otherwise stable CPA-business relationship can sour. Signals of trouble: inability to reach your accountant by phone, phone calls not returned, questions not completely answered, frequent mistakes.

Lingering dissatisfaction calls for written complaints filed with the appropriate state board of accountancy and with the AICPA. AICPA will examine the complaint and refer it to a regional trial board. If the complaint is warranted, sanctions can be levied.

State boards of accountancy handle formal complaints similarly, reviewing them, seeking a CPA's response, and providing for appeals at each step up the sometimes lengthy ladder of administrative hearings and procedures.

For the business seriously unhappy with its financial professional, another kind of professional may in the end be called for—a lawyer who can take the complaint to court.

Some Services Are Worth Asking About

As accountants move to be of greater service to their small business clients, a variety of new and old services may be available. Here's a list of some you may want to ask about:

• Maintenance of all tax records.

• Tax preparation.

• Management reporting, including data for policy and operating decisions, profit and loss statements, trend calculations and inventory information.

• Budgeting and profit planning, including long-range forecasting and break-even analysis.

• Financial controls, including credit policies and work necessary for securing outside funds.

• Corporate location, examining location needs, capital budget requirements, handling mergers and acquisitions, advising on return-on-investment considerations.

• Inventory management, such as order quantity, cost calculation and computerization.

• Personnel administration in such areas as job evaluation, recruiting, employee incentives, compensation, pension plans and employee benefits.

• Forecasting of market trends, sales and consumer attitudes.

• Marketing expense control.

• Cost accounting and reporting.

• Cost control reduction and prevention.

• Production planning and scheduling.

• Design and implementation of data processing systems for payroll, invoice and credit information.

• Clerical cost reduction.

• Analysis of filing and records management with recommendations about centralized or decentralized records and record retention methods.

• Improvements in paperwork flow and procedures manuals.

• Data maintenance, interpretation and recommendations resulting from interpretations.

• Advice on cash requirements for certain stated periods, budget forecasting, borrowing management, business organization, taxes and potential trouble spots.

• Ability to provide information on a timely and consistent basis about changes in tax laws and financial reporting requirements.

• Financial and recordkeeping software that can give you accounts receivable, order entry/invoicing and inventory management information.

• Monitoring and evaluation of revenues and expenses as compared to similar business concerns of similar size and nature.

• Invoice design.

• Training seminars or workshops on financial planning, retirement planning and other financial management issues. Seminars co-sponsored with banks or brokerage houses.

• Advice on saving an on-the-rocks concern.

• Indications of accessibility and availability.

- Computerized audits.
- Evaluation of investment opportunity.
- Computer system design.
- Surveys of client satisfaction.
- Brochures, manuals and other printed communication devices.
- Awareness of future trends affecting your business and theirs.

Action Plan For:
Selecting an Accountant

☐ Know your needs and goals first, before you seek an accountant.

☐ Consult with friends, colleagues, or business associates. Who do they recommend? Do any names come up more than others?

☐ Compare the advantages and disadvantages of using a large national firm or a small local firm.

☐ Set up a personal interview with several accountants. You want to make a choice between firms.

☐ Ask for references—and check them.

☐ Get an engagement letter from the firm you select.

Chapter Three:

Using Economic Forecasts

B usiness activities do not take place in a vacuum. Economic events beyond
your control affect your business. Your best defense is to be wary and try to
look ahead.

Economic forecasts are notoriously inexact. No two economists seem to agree
about anything—but that doesn't mean you can afford to ignore them. Even when
basic economic information is slanted or distorted for political expediency, your
competitors, suppliers and customers will shape their actions in part on their interpretation of the information.

Introduction

Macroeconomic variables, such as GNP, inflation, unemployment, interest rates,
and exchange rates, largely define our business environment. Neither size nor specialty insulates a business from the effect of these forces: "Mom and pop" gro-
cery stores, corporate manufacturing giants, neighborhood service professionals,
and multinational conglomerates are each subject to them, often in similar ways.
But occasionally these economic forces affect different businesses in conflicting
ways: An increased trade deficit, for example, means very different things to an
importer and an exporter.

Business owners and managers should try to learn as much about economic
variables as possible. The more you know, or can deduce, about future economic
conditions that affect your business, the greater your chances of preparing for, and
profiting from, those conditions.

But how do you "get the goods," that knowledge of things to come? Unfortunately, knowledge of future conditions is hard to come by at best, so we settle for a reasonable substitute—educated guesses. Some sources of data for making educated guesses are listed in Figure 3.1. Using these educated guesses for predicting future conditions is the subject of this chapter. But please keep in mind that these pages aren't intended to be a complete education in economics—just a primer to help you interpret the major economic indicators and tie them to your business.

Every business function is in some way affected by the level of, and direction of change in, economic variables. That is why you and the members of your management team should keep close track of the variables discussed in this topic and their changes, specifically, how the GNP, unemployment rate, interest rate, foreign exchange rates, and inflation affect operations, marketing, and financial management.

Economic Forecasts and Operations

The operations manager deals primarily with the physical processes used to transform materials into the product. Although the operations function is often considered insulated from external forces due to the fact that sales, finance, and other functions by nature deal more regularly with parties outside the firm, this insulation is more true by comparison than by fact.

For example, changes in the level of the Gross National Product (the value of all currently produced goods and services sold on the market during a particular time period) affect the operations manager in several ways. An increased GNP usually results in higher personal disposable income. As personal disposable income rises, the level of consumer purchases increases and creates a demand for more products and services. (This assumes, of course, that consumers' saving rates remain constant.) Production within the firm should increase, and the operations manager is wise to start arranging for increased production. If one of the materials (for example, platinum for circuit board connections) is in short supply, competition will increase for its purchase. The operations manager who can arrange a materials requirement planning program based on reliable forecasts for the firm's output will avoid headaches, either from excessive inventories of raw materials and finished goods or from work stoppages due to the lack of an essential ingredient of production. Work flow can then be planned in the smoothest, most efficient manner consistent with the demand forecast.

Further, if changes in the GNP signal sharp increases in demand for the firm's products, additional facilities or conversion to more efficient production techniques may be required. Alternatively, a drop in the GNP might suggest "tightening up the ship," to weather the coming economic storm.

Changes in the unemployment rate will determine not only the ease with which the operations manager will be able to adjust the company's work force, but also will determine the quality of the workers he or she will be able to attract and hold at a given fixed pay rate. As the unemployment rate rises, the supply of available workers increases, affording the operations manager workers with a higher level of skills at the same price. At a lower unemployment rate the operations manager may be forced to make do with less-skilled workers than he or she would normally choose.

Rising interest rates and lowered consumer demand can mean a slow inventory turnover and unnecessary financial burdens for the business.

Interest rates affect the operations manager in three ways. First, higher consumer interest rates may mean a drop in sales as credit purchases become more expensive. Production should be adjusted accordingly, expanding production if rates drop, or slowing production if interest rates increase.

Second, the tight-fisted financial manager could prevent the firm's investment in modernization or expansion programs if rising interest rates make the cost of capital greater than the return that investment can be expected to produce. The operations manager could end up nursing along an aging facility with chewing gum and hairpins, even at a time when increased production to meet increasing sales places additional demands on the equipment.

And third, interest rates determine how much inventory is ordered and carried. Rising interest rates and lowered consumer demand can mean a slow inventory turnover and unnecessary financial burdens for the business. Since lower interest rates stimulate consumer demand and reduce a business' carrying costs, increasing inventory could be a wise move for the operations manager.

The foreign exchange rate primarily affects firms whose goods and services are sold overseas. As the dollar grows stronger relative to the currency of countries buying the firm's products, the operations manager faces two challenges. Foreign sales will decrease (causing higher inventories of finished goods) as the cost of U.S.-made products climbs relative to the other country's currency. Domestic sales will also decrease as the price in dollars drops for competitive imports.

Conceivably, if the foreign competitor's increased sales are sufficient for it to increase production, competition for scarce resources may also drive up the competitor's cost and decrease their product's availability. In this case the U.S. firm would enjoy an advantage—strong dollars in a competitive, international market for resources. The operations manager might even wish to consider relocating production overseas if long-term forecasts suggest the disparity will continue for any length of time.

Figure 3.1

Sources of Economic Data

Forecasts of the five major macroeconomic variables (inflation, unemployment, GNP, interest rates, and foreign exchange rates) are available:

- Through paid subscription to commercial forecasting services;

- Free of charge from the appropriate federal government department or agency (for example, unemployment forecasts from the U.S. Bureau of Labor Statistics); and

- From your own homemade forecasting model, deductions, and educated guesses.

Virtually all of the above forecasts will rely to some extent on an underlying mathematical model or quantitative description of events that will determine the forecast outcome. Where, then, do all of those marvelous input numbers come from?

Not surprisingly, the federal government is an excellent source of such data, which is available through the Government Documents Department of your local library. Look especially for the Economic Report of the President. Published each February, the Report presents a wealth of detailed, annualized data in tables updated through the end of the previous calendar year. More detailed information on specific aspects of the national economy can be obtained by directly contacting the appropriate federal bureau or department, such as the Bureau of Labor Statistics or the Board of Governors of the Federal Reserve System.

Other sources of numerical data are probably sitting on your desk. Most business publications (such as *Business Week, Fortune, Forbes, The Economist, Money,* and even *Time)* offer an "Economics" column of some sort, such as "Index," "Forecast," "Economic Diary," "Business Outlook," "Economy and Business," and "Current Accounts." Even radio and television news broadcasts can provide up-to-date economic reporting, although you may wish to take their accompanying analyses with a grain of salt.

Finally, the regional banks of the Federal Reserve System (Atlanta, Boston, Chicago, Kansas City, Minneapolis, New York, Philadelphia, Richmond, St. Louis, and San Francisco) publish a variety of reviews and quarterlies. Most are available to the subscriber free of charge. At the national level, the monthly Federal Reserve Bulletin can be ordered from the Board of Governors and the U.S. Government Printing Office (Washington, D.C., 20402, Attention: Superintendent of Documents. Or, call the order department at 202-783-3238). These resources offer data needed to construct your own macroeconomic forecasts, as well as the latest academic research and professional thinking on the subject.

Economic Forecasts and Marketing

A business' marketing manager must find ways to get consumers to buy the company's product or service. Like the operations manager, the marketing manager must follow changes in the rate of growth of the GNP to estimate demand for the company's products. Rising GNP growth should mean higher personal consumption expenditures and more sales for the firm.

However, the marketing manager must also determine the "mix" of goods or services available for sale. A certain amount of personal disposable income must be reserved for spending on basic necessities, like food and shelter. The balance available for nonessential items may determine what features the marketing manager wishes to develop or stress in his other products. When GNP growth lags, a smaller balance of discretionary income might suggest moving toward more "practical" product features. Conversely, strong GNP growth will probably cause the consumer to shop for more "luxury" goods.

The unemployment rate will also influence how much disposable income is available for spending, although this time the relationship is inverse. If the unemployment rate rises, personal income will fall. Again, expenditures (and thus demand) for luxury items will drop, and the marketing manager will need to seek additional incentives for making the company's products attractive. A return to lower unemployment rates increases the market for purchases of discretionary items.

Interest rates affect the marketing manager primarily in the area of credit purchases. As interest rates rise for the consumer, not only will the total price (purchase price plus interest) of the marketer's products rise, making them less attractive to consumers, but consumers could start saving more given the higher returns. This increase in saving reduces disposable income available for spending.

As discussed earlier, the attractiveness of an international firm's goods in foreign markets will be affected by the exchange rate; domestic competition may heat up from imports made cheaper by a strong dollar. The marketing manager with an accurate forecast of foreign exchange rates and a firm grasp of how they will affect the company's sales can initiate damage control strategies before the damage becomes crippling. Further, the marketing manager should also watch for reverses which might suddenly make the company's products and services attractive in new markets.

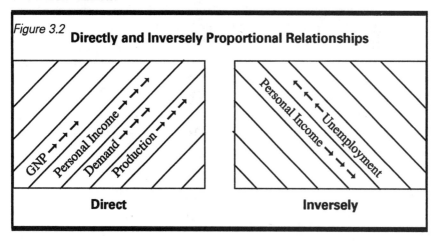

Figure 3.2 **Directly and Inversely Proportional Relationships**

Direct   **Inversely**

Economic Forecasts and Financial Management

One job of the financial manager is insuring that capital needed for production is available at the lowest cost. Cost can be measured directly as interest (rent for the use of the capital) and indirectly as opportunity costs (alternatives foregone as a result of choosing a particular course of action). To be an educated "buyer" of capital, the financial manager must closely follow the movements and relationship of economic variables.

Increases in the GNP generally signal increased demand. The financial manager will then be concerned with 1) making sure that the required capital is available at reasonable cost to finance increased production, and 2) managing surplus cash to maximize wealth. With forecasts of reduced GNP growth, the financial manager should develop strategies to counter the detrimental effects of reduced revenues.

Rising unemployment again signals a probability of reduced sales, and a possible additional problem for the financial manager. Government expenditures for unemployment compensation and other transfer payments affected by unemployment will increase; the government's appetite for capital will grow. This appetite can only be satisfied in three ways: an increase in corporate taxes (which come right out of a company's cash flow and directly reduce the undistributed profits available for reinvestment); an increase in personal taxes (reducing personal disposable income available for buying the company's products); or deficit financing (when the government competes with the business sector for investment dollars and drives up interest rates).

To be an educated "buyer" of capital, the financial manager must closely follow the movements and relationship of economic variables.

Rising interest rates affect the financial manager not only by increasing the cost of capital, but also by altering the time horizon for investment decisions. With stable rates, investors will be more willing to commit funds to long-term debt at fixed rates of return. Under erratic or sharply rising rates, the investor can be less confident that a required rate of return will be earned by the end of the investment period, and so a higher (or perhaps a "floating") rate will be charged to counter the uncertainty. In such cases, it might pay the financial manager to look more closely at short-term financing. Reliable forecasts are necessary to insure that the firm is not locked in to a high interest rate when the "rent" on capital starts dropping. Alternatively, the manager armed with forecasts of rising rates might wish to lock in his financing before the cost of capital starts to rise.

Figure 3.3

What Do the Leading Economic Indicators Really Indicate?

Once every month, like clockwork, the nation's newspapers carry stories of changes in the leading economic indicators as reported by The U.S. Commerce Department. The leading indicators are followed closely by business executives and other decision makers. When the indicators change significantly they signal that the economy is likely to change. In other words, the leading indicators are presumed to lead the economy and forecast where it is going. They are also important factors in determining the five macroeconomic variables discussed in this topic.

The leading indicator approach to forecasting relies on detecting those indicators that consistently lead the business cycle by at least a few months. The Commerce Department has selected twelve such indicators:

1. Number of hours in the average workweek. Changing the hours of work for existing employees is a first step before changing the number of employed persons.

2. Number of initial claims for unemployment insurance. First claims by the newly unemployed indicate subsequent unemployment down the road.

3. Volume of manufacturers' new orders. New orders precede final sales to consumers.

4. Vendor performance. Slower deliveries of raw materials may indicate greater sales of raw materials and subsequent greater sales of finished goods.

5. Net business formation. Today's new businesses represent tomorrow's new production.

6. Volume of contracts and orders for plant and equipment. Intentions to invest precede actual investment.

7. New building permits. Housing construction begins with permits to build.

8. Volume of inventories on hand and on order. Businesses build up inventory when they expect future sales to be brisk.

9. Change in sensitive material prices. A rise in materials prices signals increased demand for materials and increased production of finished goods in the near future.

10. Stock market prices. Stock prices reflect the market's consensus of expected economic activity in the future. When the market moves up, the economy is expected to improve.

11. The money supply. Monetary expansions and contractions are known to precede overall economic expansions and contractions due to the lag in the effect of monetary policy.

12. Change in credit outstanding. Production often requires advance financing.

The financial manager's main concern with exchange rates is how much capital flows into and out of U.S. investments. A strong dollar attracts foreign investment to the U.S., increasing funds available for investment and possibly reducing interest rates. A weak dollar has the opposite effect, and could cause interest rates to rise.

Inflation: Its Effect on Operations, Marketing, and Finance

Inflation is an increase in prices, and the inflation rate is the percent rise in those prices. Deflation is a decrease in prices, while disinflation is a slowdown in the rate of price increases. For the operations manager, as for the marketing and financial managers, a rise in the inflation rate should forewarn a decrease in demand for nonessential services and goods.

For example, an apple (representing a fixed income) can be cut in two pieces. If one piece becomes bigger (nondiscretionary purchases under inflation and fixed income), the second piece necessarily becomes smaller. This is further aggravated by increased prices: Since each purchase takes a bigger bite out of the whole, the consumer will be able to make fewer purchases. This is because of the inversely proportional relationship of the consumer's purchases of essential to nonessential services and goods, given a fixed personal income. Thus, wage controls without price controls (or transfer payments like Social Security or food stamps) which fail to rise at a rate consistent with that of inflation is indeed a cruel policy.

However, if the apple is allowed to expand at the same rate as the bites, there is no relative change. In this case, inflation would have little effect other than a devaluation of the currency in real terms. Unfortunately, inflation rarely (if ever) affects all sectors of the economy equally. Some industries (for example, oil products-based manufacturing in 1974) are crippled by rising prices in certain commodities. In addition, every business will feel the effects of inflation—on labor and materials costs, for example—differently.

Think of dropping stones (representing changes in prices) into a river (representing the U.S. economy). Since these stones vary in their size and location, the cumulative effect of the ripples (a company's individual vulnerability to all of the individual changes in prices) will depend upon the company's size and proximity to the stones, and the way in which the ripples interact. Therefore, every business owner must determine the business' own susceptibility to inflation.

A business' manager should therefore interpret inflation rates as a lawyer might interpret "general rules," and look to specific shocks as "exceptions." A rising inflation rate generally points to a reduction in consumer purchases of discretionary services and products. The operations manager of firms in such industries needs to scale back production. The marketing manager needs to look for ways to make the product more desirable to the consumer, either by changing the product's features, by lowering the purchase price, or by extending credit. The financial manager can count on paying a higher "rent" for the use of investors' money. In periods of inflation, the investor will demand a higher than usual rate of return for long-term investments, since the investment will be paid back with dollars worth less than those invested. As before, the financial manager should consider turning his or her attention toward short-term markets to meet capital needs during inflation.

During deflation, the consumer can purchase more goods with a given personal income. The production manager needs to start insuring that various ingredients for production will be available for increased output. The marketing manager faces a dilemma: The value the business receives for goods or services is less than that under previous stable prices. Should prices be raised while all around competitors' prices may be falling? Market share would fall dramatically, as would sales revenues. The financial manager would start howling. At the same time that revenues were dropping, each dollar taken in from sales would be worth less, creating a need for more and more sources of capital. The only saving grace would be that the firm's purchases would cost less, reducing the total amount of capital needed for the firm's production.

And here is where the error in the analogy of an apple as fixed personal income becomes glaringly apparent. Personal income cannot remain constant during periods of inflation and deflation, given stable employment. Not only does inflation determine the size of the slices, it greatly contributes to the size of the pie (GNP) as well.

Now, just to make things confusing, let's say that the unemployment rate fluctuates. With a high real GNP, firms will need more production workers. Unemployment will drop, but wages will rise. This expense will be passed on in the form of higher prices to the consumer and will fuel inflation. On the other hand, low real GNP would reduce the need for workers, raising the unemployment rate while slowing inflation.

Thus, the user of forecasts of macroeconomic variables must also consider the interaction of economic variables. (See Figure 3.4) A failure to do so could mean developing an inappropriate strategy for tackling the business conditions the forecast predicts.

Summary

Forecasting the economy is an important part of business planning. If you have sound notions about what's going to happen in the future, you can plan ahead to maximize the use of borrowed funds, gauge production to meet your customers'

Figure 3.4

How Certain Economic Variables Interact

Macroeconomic variables interact with each other in a variety of ways under different conditions. Some interactions are well understood and can be predicted through common sense. One such interplay, described as the Fisher Effect, predicts that as inflation rises, interest rates will undoubtedly follow, as lenders seek to enhance their returns from less valuable dollars.

Unfortunately, other relations are less clear. For example, if inflation in this country rises and causes higher prices of American products relative to imports, then the dollar's value could drop, since demand for foreign currencies to buy cheaper foreign goods would increase. Alternatively, wouldn't a rising U.S. inflation rate cause U.S. interest rates to climb as well (through the Fisher Effect), thereby strengthening the dollar as it becomes a more appealing investment to foreigners?

Your answer will depend upon your view of the business environment and the school of economic thinking you choose to apply. Are you a Keynesian or a Monetarist? A Demand—or a Supply-Sider? A Neoclassical thinker or a Marxist?

Beyond that determination, there are a number of tricks you can apply to make your forecasting job easier. First, try to determine which change is the cause and which is the effect. Second, try to differentiate between short-term and long-term reactions. Finally, separate strong effects from weak ones; you might even quantify the size of the effect by using your own "scale" to represent the strength of the variables' relationship. When you're finished, add up all of the pluses and minuses to see which direction you think the affected variable will go.

In short, break the problem up into bite-sized pieces, chew on them a little, apply a little common sense, and you will probably develop an economic forecast at least as good as that of the experts.

demands, and make the most of new markets, new sources of labor, and new product lines.

But since your time is undoubtedly best spent running your business, take advantage of what experts offer. Talk to your banker, accountant, and trade association—they can help analyze what economic trends mean to your business and industry. And, try to use some of the resources listed in Figure 3.1 of this topic. Keeping up-to-date with economists' predictions will hone your judgment skills.

Action Plan For:
Using Economic Forecasts

☐ Monitor forecasts of the five major macroeconomic variables: Inflation, Unemployment, GNP (or GDP: Gross Domestic Product), Interest Rates, and Foreign Exchange Rates.

☐ Assess the implications of these forecasts on Operations, Marketing, and Finance.

Chapter Four:

Financing

....

F inancing a business is a simple enough concept: You must have adequate funds to enable your business to start, expand, and continue operations. The fact that funds are needed is the simple part. Where they come from is another matter.

The purpose of this topic is to explain the various types of financing needed for different purposes by most small businesses. We will also identify the sources of these funds. You must know how much you need of each type before you can start looking for places to get it.

Understanding the types and sources of financing will help you to avoid the four most common abuses of business funds:

1. Undercapitalization.

2. Excess debt.

3. Insufficient use of credit.

4. Friday night financing.

This list is by no means exhaustive. New ways to fritter away the resources of any business manage to turn up regularly. The most common is lack of financial controls, which is apt to lead to a nickel and dime erosion.

Abuse of financing is somewhat different. One difference is that it proceeds on a more dramatic scale. Another is that while controls may be imposed at some later date and the bleeding of money slowed and stopped, the damage from financial error is much more critical and lasting.

Small businesses are almost always undercapitalized or slimly capitalized, and are much more susceptible to the negative impact of a substantial mistake than larger organizations which have the financial resources to absorb more than one major error.

Financing does not—and must not—take place apart from other aspects of your operation, or separate from your business plan. In fact, financing is the heart of your operation and your business plan. It affects every part of your operation.

Small businesses have few fixed points by which to measure progress. Your financial plan provides one of the best benchmarks possible. Financing plans are expressed in dollars. Operations can be measured in dollars—then compared against the plan.

Remember that there are two parties involved in any financing effort—the business seeking the financing and the financier.

This is important to keep in mind because all too often a giant communication problem develops between the small business principals and their financing sources. You can avoid such problems.

Bankers and those who handle other people's money are obliged, both legally and morally, to protect their depositors' money—it is NOT their responsibility to make loans. A bank is not allowed to take high risks. While your business ideas may sound wonderful and attractive, a bank must place the funds of its depositors into reasonably safe and secured investments, or run afoul of a stringent body of laws. All lenders must ask: "How will this loan be repaid?" If there is no clear answer to this question, then the loan should not be made.

Identify Different Needs for Funds Within the Business

This step does not, repeat does not, involve money. One of the most dangerous errors small business owners make is to begin with a sum of dollars in mind as a borrowing target.

If you are starting a business, for example, you can probably list the greater portion of capital assets you will need. Included in such a list could be store fixtures, start-up costs of lease deposits, delivery equipment, office machinery and furniture, operating equipment, and real estate. Picture your business. Spread it out like a photograph in your mind's eye. Those assets which will be the basis of your business, the fixed assets, are the capital assets. While they will be described on your balance sheet in dollar terms, they are, essentially, physical items. Some intangibles may creep in, such as copyrights and patents, but the physical plant and related equipment are the first part of the business to understand.

Notice that no dollars have yet entered the considerations. The needs come first, then their timing and duration. For example: You have an ongoing need for a place to do business, say a factory if you're a manufacturer. Then you need equipment to make whatever your product is—drill presses, turret lathes, tools to keep them going, and so forth. You also need materials—but here the need is of a different duration. You buy material, use it up in a short period, sell the finished product, buy more material, and so on. You have begun to enter the realm of the current asset. And the ways to finance current assets are different.

Unhappily, most people go from "Let me see how much I can raise. . . " to "What will I do with the money?" and never address themselves to the basic question: *"What business needs must be met?"*

Ignoring this is one reason so many small businesses fail. Identify the needs, then—if you cannot finance the resolution of those needs properly—decide what to do. Don't jump in before you know what you're jumping into or you'll go broke.

Capital assets are expected to be paid for principally from invested capital, secondarily from the proceeds of long-term loans. *It is important to tie debt life to asset life.* Short-term needs should be covered by short-term debt. Long-term or capital needs should be covered by long-term debt or invested capital.

How Much Money Is Needed?

The triple approach of high/low/most likely works well here. For every contemplated purchase or investment, try to put a dollar figure onto it which reflects an unlimited budget, a survival budget, and the most likely figure: one which is somewhat above survival but well below extravagance.

To arrive at a rough approximation of your capital needs you must calculate the following:

(1) Your capital asset costs—plant, equipment, supplies, materials, opening inventories, perhaps other costs as well if they are capitalized.

(2) The deepest (largest) negative cash flow—and this is only found by pushing a cash flow projection out far enough to be sure that you will have adequate operating positive cash flow to carry on normal business operations. This will be a particularly important exercise if you are entering a period of sharp growth. See Chapter Five for more on this.

(3) A safety margin. Your accountant can help with all of these, but you must be the one to provide the insight into your business.

Then, add (1), (2) and (3). This will give you a rough total of the capital you need. If anything, it will call for more capital than is absolutely necessary. Fine, you can adjust later—but the added safety factor represented by overcapitalization helps you sleep nights. You won't kill your business by having too much capital. You will kill it, eventually, by having too little.

The other approach is for all other financing purposes. Begin by identifying the needs, then place high, low and most likely costs against those needs. This is one of the times to ask, once again, the basic question: *"Do we really need this?"*

If the need stands up and the dollar cost is not out of reach, then you are in position once again to know— not merely guess— how much money you must raise.

This is another danger point. All too often the glittering spectacle of acquiring a new toy outweighs prudence. Make sure that the acquisition (whether of a thing or a service or a skill) will be justified in terms of achieving your business' objectives. By knowing how much it will cost, you have a partial handle on this judgment. Without planning, you'll end up with enough debt to get you in trouble but not enough credit to get you out again. Be conservative.

What Kind of Money Is Needed?

The second most common financing error (following undercapitalization) is securing the wrong kind of financing. The variety of ways to do this is almost endless.

If the purpose of a loan is seasonal, it must be paid off seasonally. If it is stretched out to a long-term loan, then the next year the same problem—though worse—will arise. The parallel here is to consumer debt: Waldo gets behind on his monthly bills, so he gets a debt consolidation loan. He now spreads repayment of short-term debt needs over a long term; this makes his cash flow look pretty good until he gets deeper into debt (he hasn't changed the consumption pattern that got him in this bind in the first place). So he has to reconsolidate. And re-reconsolidate. And so forth. The hole just gets deeper and deeper and the monthly payments bigger and bigger.

A business is no different. Recurrent loan needs are best handled by a financing vehicle designed for that kind of need.

The other side of this coin is trying to finance long-term needs, say for fixed asset acquisition, over a short term, by abusing a non-revolving line of credit This will drain off working capital with gruesome haste, and can make growth impossible. It is also likely to destroy your reputation for paying your bills and servicing your debt. If you expect to use that expensive turret lathe for the next ten years, then don't try to pay for it in six months. A term loan for four years or so might be the best way to go.

Now: Whether the need is for debt or for capital you must consider the cost. One reason for the repeated warning against carrying too much debt is that the cost of that money, the interest and the principal repayment, may exceed the return you can earn after expenses on that money. This is a fine way to slowly go broke, almost painless until suddenly there's no working capital (except illiquid receivables) and no credit.

High debt-to-worth ratios (high leverage) can show spectacular returns on invested capital But if things don't work out— and they seldom do (the best laid plans . . .)—then the loss figures are also spectacular, and net worth vanishes.

Too little capital will rapidly surface as negative net worth—and the only remedy for negative net worth is new investment. In most cases, financing sources are wary of lending into a negative net worth situation. Would you want to invest in a company whose management lacked the basic foresight to properly capitalize its business—and then ran it at a loss to boot? Of course not. Yet that is exactly what many borrowers expect lenders to do!

Figure the cost. If you usually net 5% on gross sales, and debt costs your company 15-18%, then that cost must be justified in terms of increased sales, increased efficiency, greater profits, or all three. Otherwise it merely becomes an added burden. One excellent safeguard here for retailers is found in the sales/worth ratio. If your sales/worth ratio is higher than trade averages, then you're overtrading—making a small amount of capital work overtime. This is a risky disease. The cure is more capital—not more debt.

Your banker and accountant can help you here. You will be doubly protected, however, by looking *before* you go to your financing sources for what kind of financing makes the most sense for you, both now and in the long run. Expedience will hurt you. Take a relatively conservative path and you'll do yourself and your investors a favor.

Credit and debt, properly used, enable you to grow faster than an ultra-conservative no-debt strategy. Not to use financing is about as sane as playing baseball but never batting—pure defensiveness is ultimately self-defeating. There's a middle course between excessive debt and ultra-conservatism that's difficult to steer. It all starts by identifying legitimate business needs.

When Is It Needed?

Identify the timing. Plan ahead and set specific dates.

A common error in small business circles is to leave financing needs until the last moment, that moment at which they become so pressing that a slight hitch in securing financing can seriously damage the business.

Once you know what kind of money and how much money is needed, then and only then can you start setting up a timetable, a plan.

For example: A line of credit for a new company may take several month to be approved and in place, whereas a well-established company might get the same line for the same purposes over the phone. A real estate deal will almost always take three weeks or longer; the legalities alone make that a sure bet. A term loan may have to wait for an evaluation of the equipment being financed. A construc-

Figure 4.1

Friday Night Financing

Friday Night Financing: Late on Friday afternoon a harried business owner darts into his bank, corners his banker, and says he needs some debt money NOW. Not Monday. NOW.

It's a sign of poor managerial judgment and planning, as well as a clear warning that the loan is probably hastily conceived with an inordinately high degree of risk attached.

tion or a progress loan will have a built-in timetable but never take less than several weeks to negotiate. And so it goes. Visit your banker well before you need him and ask for the timing on the kind of loan you may need. He'll happily tell you. So will your accountant. By seeing your banker *before* you desperately need his help, you avoid the Friday Night Financing problem.

Set the dates, then follow them. You can always slow down a loan, but you cannot speed up a loan. The same holds true for equity investors. Getting them eager is more difficult than discouraging them.

If you know that in a year added capital for growth is going to be needed, and that capital will not be generated from operating profits, start hunting up new capital now, before you panic. Investors need time to think—and if that time need puts you in a hard place, you'll either not get the financing, or the financing will be more costly (in terms of equity or control or interest) than it needs to be.

Develop a Financing Plan

Part of your strategy is to make sure that you and your financing prospects keep in touch, during lean times as well as prosperous times. Get your financiers to visit you at your place. This lets them get a feel for your business in a physical way, gives you the home-court advantage, and even lets them offer comments and suggestions. This kind of advice can be tremendously helpful.

Your financing proposal will vary with your relationship to your sources of financing. If you are well-established, you will need no more than updated financial statements and a statement of intended use and source of repayment of your debt. For a new or rapidly growing business, a more comprehensive plan is necessary—and then it should be updated periodically, whether you need more financing from outside or not. A good plan is a lot of work and will take a lot of time—but the benefits are guaranteed to far outweigh these considerations.

Your aim is to keep your sources of financing favorably aware of your progress towards clearly defined business objectives. In a word: credibility.

A banker's aim is protection of depositors' money. The banker's prime concern: How will the loan be repaid?

The investor's aim is to achieve either a satisfactory percentage return on capital investment or to achieve a good capital gain, or both. Honesty with your banker and other financiers is not just the best policy; it's the only policy.

Everyone—including your other financing sources—wants to earn a return on his or her money that is in line with the amount of risk. Ordinarily, a low risk investment won't generate high returns. A high risk is taken in hopes of high return, though it may be almost as chancy as investing in the sweepstakes. Keep the source of the money in mind as you prepare the initial proposal.

All of this will give you a good chance at securing financing of the right kind from the right sources. However, if this fails, then what?

You need a back-up plan. You can't just assume that your first plan will work—so cultivate more than one financing source, as the case may dictate. The basic information will be the same (what is the need, what is the amount, how will it be paid off), but the slant may differ.

You might also want to form two alternative strategies: a capital conservative plan and a more highly leveraged plan. If you could bootstrap your business, but it would pinch your growth, putting the two plans side-by-side will almost always encourage your banker to give you the credit you need for maximum safe growth. Good financial planning is a key indicator of managerial competence.

Implement and Review

Securing and applying the financing is only the beginning. While a bad financing decision will have long-lasting and deep-rooted effects, good plans become poor plans unless they are reviewed and recast periodically. Don't hang onto last year's plans too long because time brings change. Habits form all too easily—in business financing, as well as in other areas.

Do enough planning to make sure you don't botch the financing—either by not getting it or by the all too human process of mistaking securing a loan for business success. This often happens: A business secures a medium-term loan for working capital purposes, a legitimate and appropriate use of debt, but the owner promptly goes out and buys a few goodies for the business, forgetting the working capital needs. A bloated cash supply must be checked by a written plan of what to do with the loan proceeds. Don't fall victim to this kind of error. You made your plan based on purely business considerations; follow it.

Since your financing needs are ongoing (if you stay in business and aren't hyper-conservative, the odds are you'll use trade credit and bank financing on a regular basis), your plan should be reviewed at least annually, preferably more often. There is a built-in bonus in all this. Once formulated, your financing plan becomes an integral part of your budget/control process. Used in this manner you will be tuned to the need for changes, both negative and positive, on a regular basis, and will be able to respond to these needs to your maximum benefit.

Summary

By carefully analyzing your financing needs and expressing them in an objective way, you avoid problems caused by inadequate capitalization, excessive debt, poor use of the powerful tool of credit (both trade and other debt), and Friday Night Financing attempts which either fail or make you fail. Good financial management follows from a clear understanding of how and why money takes different shapes and fills different purposes in your business—and good financial management leads to better and more profitable business.

Glossary: Financial Terms

Capital: Capital funds are those funds which are needed for the base of the business. Usually they are put into the business in a fairly permanent form such as in fixed assets, plant and equipment, or are used in other ways which are not recoverable in the short run unless you sell the entire business.

Working Capital: This is the difference between current assets and current liabilities. Contrasted with **capital**, a permanent use of funds, **working capital** is for relatively short-term use. Working capital cycles through your business in a variety of forms: inventories, accounts and notes receivable, cash and securities, prepaid expenses. Working capital may fluctuate in terms of seasonal needs.

Debt: Debt refers to borrowed funds, whether from your own coffers, from other individuals, banks or other institutions. It is generally secured with a note, which in turn may be secured by a lien against property or other assets. Ordinarily, the note states repayment and interest provisions, which vary greatly in both amount and duration, depending upon the purpose, source and terms of the loan. Some debt is **convertible**, that is, it may be changed into direct ownership of a portion of a business under certain stated conditions.

Equity: Equity is the owner's investment in the business. Unlike capital, equity is what remains after the liabilities of the company are subtracted from the assets—thus it may be greater than or less than the capital invested in the business. Equity investment carries with it a share of ownership and usually a share in profits, as well as some say in how the business is managed.

Term Loans: Either secured or unsecured, usually for periods of more than a year to as many as twenty years. Term loans are paid off like a mortgage: so many dollars per month for so many years. The most common uses of term loans are for equipment and other fixed asset purposes, for working capital, and for real estate.

Subordinated Debt: Subordinated debt is sometimes referred to as "quasi-capital" because it serves the same purposes as capital as far as a bank is concerned. Subordinating debt means placing that particular debt behind bank debt— that is, should your business go bust and have to be sold for asset value, your bank gets paid before the holder of the subordinated debt.

Loan Agreement: A document which states what a business can or cannot do as long as it owes money to (usually) a bank. A loan agreement may place restrictions on the owner's salary, on dividends, on amount of other debt, on working capital limits, on sales, or number of added personnel.

Note: The basic business loan, a note, represents a loan which will be repaid, or substantially reduced 30, 60, or 90 days later at a stated interest rate. These are short-term, and unless they are made under a line of credit, a separate loan application is needed for each loan and each renewal.

Loans: Debt money for small business is usually in the form of bank loans, loans which in a real sense are personal loans because a new small business is hard to evaluate in terms of credit-worthiness and degree of risk. A **secured** loan is a loan which is backed up by a claim against some asset or assets of a business. An **unsecured** loan is backed up by the faith the bank has in the borrower's ability to pay the money back.

Line of Credit: Either secured or unsecured, an agreement which ordinarily is renewed on an annual basis where a bank holds funds available for the use of a business. Usually an unsecured line will have to be completely paid out once a year.

Revolving Line of Credit: Similar to a line of credit, except it needn't be paid out annually. This kind of loan is of particular interest to a rapidly growing company with weak capitalization—and may be converted to a term loan under certain conditions.

Action Plan For:
Financing

☐ Identify different needs for funds within the business. What needs require cash from outside the business? What can be financed from operations? What will be financed?

☐ Determine how much money is needed. Be specific.

☐ Decide what kind of money is needed: debt or new capital; short term or long term? permanent capital or temporary debt?

☐ Determine ahead of time when you need the money.

☐ Develop a financing plan to anticipate and answer your bankers' or other investors' questions. Go over your plan with them; solicit and respond to their ideas and advice.

☐ Implement your financial plan. Review it as needed, at least annually if not more often.

Chapter Five:

Forecasting and Cash Flow Budgeting

....

Your financial statements operate as a kind of distant early warning system when carefully prepared and used. In the previous chapter, Financing, the importance of a cash flow projection was tied not only to figuring out how much money was needed but also when that money was needed. The projected P&L (aka Income Statement) helps identify how the loan will be repaid.

These statements work together. You use the P&L projection to determine profitability; this provides the basis for a detailed cash flow pro forma which in turn becomes your budget. It also is the basis for your financing plan, the best means of testing the feasibility of your business goals, and a key element in the survival of your business.

If you could have only one financial statement to guide you, I'd suggest it should be the cash flow budget. It is the most important financial statement you can have—it models your business, provides the necessary checks and balances and financial controls to guide performance, wins bankers' hearts, and keeps spending and investment impulses under control.

Anyone can set a budget, but only an exceptionally good manager can set a budget that works—and that works not only as a necessary cash control, but also as a positive means to attain your business goals.

Forecasting and budgeting are so closely related that they can't be separated. Your forecasts become your budget. And since the process of forecasting fills so many people with confusion and/or dread, this chapter attempts to break forecasting into a series of manageable steps.

Once you have made your sales and expense forecasts, the actual budgeting process is simple—but if your forecasts are out of line, your budget will not serve any useful purpose. Your budgeting and forecasting stand or fall together. Unless radically unforeseeable events impact on your business (which is rare), you'll get more and more accurate with experience.

Preparing a forecasting/budgeting system is one of the most difficult yet most important tasks you face as a business owner. The budget is the basic tool of the manager who looks to the future and prepares for what is in store.

Would you start out on a trip before deciding on a destination? Once the destination is determined, would you start off before mapping out the best route? Of course not! The same holds true for your business. A well thought-out financial plan, or budget, will help you set and evaluate both the goals to be reached and the directions to be followed. By putting your plan in writing, you will be in the best possible position to improve your forecasting and budgeting skills—and your company's profits.

How do you go about the daunting task of forecasting?

First, **set broad guidelines and goals** to be achieved during the budget period—and beyond. These guidelines and goals will become more precise as your forecasting/budgeting proceeds. Don't try to start out with your goals fine-tuned.

Second, **review current business conditions** and carefully examine the facts and figures pertaining to your business. You prepare your forecast or projection to assist you in determining the goals of your enterprise, but those goals must be realistic. As you zero in on your precise objectives and forecasts, rethink your business practices and policies. (These are still broad, non-detailed considerations—but important.)

With your goals set and strategies in mind, your budget tells you what it will take to reach your desired profit level. The road to business success is full of pitfalls and potential setbacks. How you handle these problems will be covered in the budget; at the very least, you need positive cash flow to survive. This is why you budget.

You should keep one eye on the present operations of your business and the other looking out for future trends. This is not easy, especially if your business is heading in one direction while trends are pointing in the other.

For example, consider the plight of the tourist industry when travel was restricted by the cost and shortage of gas. The OPEC mess was not a surprise—yet many tourist oriented businesses unwisely expanded even as the crisis deepened.

To operate your business effectively, you must know what is happening around you. Determine what factors affect all businesses and then focus in on events that will have the most direct effect on yours. With this knowledge in mind, plan accordingly.

Management's first job is to maintain the profitable survival of the business—and this may require reducing the size of the business and its level of sales.

If you expect a gas crisis, for example, don't enlarge your tourist-oriented business. Play it safe. Retrench. Successful entrepreneurs are aware of the general business outlook and how it will affect their concerns. No forecasts are 100% accurate. However, many events that affect your business are known and can be planned for well in advance. A new shopping center, new road construction, altered bus routes, new housing developments, and similar events are proposed long before their effects are felt. Everyone in business should have been prepared for the increased payroll and FICA taxes and the health care cost crisis. We knew these changes were coming and, therefore, we should have prepared for them.

Prepare a Profit and Loss Projection

The first step in your forecast is the projection of an annual profit and loss statement, broken down by sales and expense categories.

Your P&L projection is for a year (or for the proposed period of your budget). Since it covers a full business cycle, don't worry about seasonal fluctuations, collecting receivables, or that large reduction of an outstanding loan—you'll cover these contingencies later, when you push the cash flow projection. Don't try to break it out month by month or you'll drown in details you can't use.

This P&L projection is not intended to be a fine-tuned, fully spelled out financial statement. It is a guide, an approximation to help you arrive at an accurate forecast of sales and expenses. After you have gone through the complete budgeting process, you can make it more accurate, and may wish to project a monthly or quarterly P&L for control purposes.

The first question to ask yourself is: **What sales can I expect to generate in the coming months?** We suggest you do this with the help of the form entitled **Profit and Loss Projection**.

The format of the P&L projection is given in Figure 5.1 below. You may wish to modify it to fit your particular operation, but do not change its basic form. Used properly, this worksheet will assist you in predicting future profits.

Forecast Sales

The form is simple to use—what may take some doing is to let your imagination loose. During the course of the next year, what are the lowest sales figures you could expect? What are the highest? Approach the projection one step at a time, and avoid the problem of trying to do everything at once.

Be reasonable. When this form was first used by one of our clients, the worst figure given was $0, the best, $1,000,000. Try approaching it this way: What was your worst year recently? Your best? What was the worst single drop in sales from one period to the next? The best increase?

To forecast sales, break down your sales by product lines (or services). Then predict the worst case and the best case, making notes on your assumptions. If you have historical sales records available, this will not be too arduous—but if your business is a startup, or in a period of rapid expansion or flux, it will be more difficult.

That's understandable. But do it anyway. A rough guide to the future will help you establish more accurate guides later. You need some benchmarks to measure your progress.

Take into account normal growth patterns, inflation, the impact of major changes in your business or industry—then establish your P&L projection for the budget period.

This mode of attack helps you think in realistic terms. All you want to establish here are parameters, boundaries to think within.

The left-hand column is used to project a bare bones profit and loss statement. Start by projecting sales assuming the worst conditions. If you have more than one line of goods, then identify each line. You'll want to be able to cull out the losers and encourage your more profitable efforts.

Remember, this is the worst possible situation. Be gloomy—assume that you'll have bad weather, poor traffic, lazy salespeople. Perhaps you'll have shortages of products, disrupted delivery schedules, cancelled orders. This is a "what-if" effort, so don't be alarmed. Sometimes it helps to take this dismal view—you may be able to identify potential soft spots in your operation. (Perhaps a competitor is going to invade your market or you won't get that contract renewal. What then?)

In the column to the right, project sales under the best possible conditions. This will be your most optimistic forecast of revenues.

This is more fun. All your sales efforts will succeed, customers will beat down your door, suppliers will meet schedules so you'll never have a stock-out. Your ads will be 100% effective. This commercial utopia is about as likely as the gloomy one above—but both have been known to happen.

Eighty percent of your profits probably come from 20% of sales.

Can you identify your winning products?

Next year's winners? Declining products?

Forecast Expenses

Next, identify all expenses that will be incurred to generate the revenues under the low and high sales projections.

The best way to gather this information is to review past operating statements and your business records. A going concern incurs expenses throughout the year. No matter what the level of production or sales, there will still be some costs. Those costs that are present and remain fairly constant at any level of output are called **fixed** expenses.

Expenses that increase or decrease with production are **variable** expenses. As sales volume increases and decreases, variable expenses increase and decrease. If there is no output, there will be no variable expenses. At zero production, only fixed expenses are incurred. For example:

Variable Costs	**Fixed Costs**
Cost of goods sold	Rent/mortgage payments
Cost of sales	Office expenses
Advertising	Certain taxes
Labor & sales force	Owners' salaries & withdrawals
Variable utilities	Leased equipment payments
Shop expense	Fixed basic telephone/utilities

Each expense that your business incurs should be carefully examined. This is an education in itself. Which expenses can be justified? Which expenses can be lowered? Increased? An expense lowered by one dollar with no change in sales will increase profit by the same one dollar. On the other hand, increasing certain expenses can often improve sales and increase profits.

As you identify all expenses as either fixed or variable, you should start to get an idea of what it takes to make your business run better. Profits get devoured by unnecessary expenses—in all businesses.

Fixed expenses will remain more or less the same under both the worst

Figure 5.1

**Preparation of
Profit & Loss Projection**

1. **Project Annual Sales**
   A. Left-hand column—
      worst possible conditions

2. **Project Annual Expenses—
   Worst and Best Conditions**
   A. Fixed expenses
   B. Variable expenses
      1. Fixed % variable expenses
      2. All other variable expenses

3. **Compare "worst" and "best"
   projections, prepare reasonable
   forecast with figures
   somewhere in between, and
   review.**

Figure 5.2

How Do You Identify Expenses That Are Too High Or Too Low?

Seek out industry averages for your line of business. Some libraries can get this kind of information for you and your accountant or banker should be able to help. Ask for the Robert Morris Associates material.

In highly individual businesses with no comparable industry ratios available, look for others who are in the same line of business, but not directly competitive. Trade notes with them—and try not to be too nervous about competition. Sometimes a business school can act as intermediary.

Failing 1 and 2, tinker. Weigh the effect of each category, especially advertising and sales expenses. These are apt to be the trouble spots, as they are somewhat intangible, and get abused.

and best situations. Once you have identified which expense categories are fixed in your business, you can record the proper amount in the left- and right-hand columns. Be particularly aware of the expenses that remain constant only to a certain volume of production. For example, a payment for leased equipment may remain constant until volume requires the move to larger equipment and a higher lease payment. Fixed expenses are fixed only within broad limits; if sales go way up, you may need more salespeople, more office help, and more debt. All of these can affect your fixed costs dramatically. (And training costs for expansion will become burdensome. Ask any manufacturer who relies on skilled help.)

Variable expenses increase as sales and production increase. When projecting variable expenses, many categories will remain a constant percentage of sales. Freight, postage, cost of goods sold, and operating supplies fall into this category. For many businesses, the same holds true for telephone, laundry, and auto expense.

Some variable expenses do not remain a constant percentage of sales. Payroll, for example, will increase only at certain sales levels. There is a minimum work force required in most businesses. A new employee is added only when needed— that is, when production reaches the point where the present work force is unable to keep up with demand. Payroll and payroll taxes will increase only as volume requires the increase.

In many businesses, advertising will remain a constant percentage of sales to a point where the expense will level off. Or it may be necessary to make a drastic increase in advertising to take over a large share of the market.

Other expenses that fall into this uncertain variable category are utilities, repairs and maintenance, auto and truck expense, and purchase of fixed assets. And please note that miscellaneous expense is not a catch-all for those disbursements that you don't know what to do with. Suggestion: If miscellaneous expense is greater than 3% of sales, break these expenses down into smaller categories.

Figure 5.3

Profit & Loss Projection

		Low	Most Likely	High
Sales	Product/Service Line A........			
	Product/Service Line B........			
	Product/Service Line C........			
	Product/Service Line D........			
Total Sales Revenue				
Cost of	Line A..............................			
Goods Sold	Line B			
	Line C			
	Line D..............................			
	Total Cost of Goods Sold...			
	Gross Profit			
Expenses*				
Variable	Payroll..............................			
	Sales Commissions			
	Freight..............................			
	Travel and Entertainment			
	Sales Tax..............................			
Semi—Variable	Advertising and Promotion..			
	FICA/ Payroll Taxes			
	Supplies..............................			
	Telephone			
	Auto and Transport..............			
	Postage..............................			
	Payroll..............................			
	Interest			
	Insurance..............................			
Fixed	Dues and Subscriptions........			
	Bank Charges......................			
	Rent..............................			
	Utilities			
	Property Taxes			
	Office Expenses			
	Total Expenses			
	Profit Before Depreciation			
	Depreciation			
	Net Profit			

* The expense items have been somewhat arbitrarily assigned to fixed, semi-variable, and variable categories. Expense items for your business may differ. Ask your accountant if you have questions.

Don't worry too much about making the fixed/variable decision—when in doubt, consider the expense fixed. This will force a conservative forecast. For almost every small business, such conservatism is highly desirable.

Comparison and Review

Once you have prepared a projected profit and loss statement assuming the worst and best conditions, make a comparison. In the center column of your form, prepare a projection assuming figures somewhere in between "worst" and "best." This results in a more realistic forecast.

Take the time to test your projection. Recognizing the potential and/or limitations of your business is critical to the success of your venture. Is the demand in the market great enough so that the desired sales level can be reached? Is the production capacity of your business adequate to produce the desired profit level? Break down sales into units, then units per person, then units per day. Apply the test now—it will save you much time and money later.

We call this the bowl-of-soup test, after a customer who needed to achieve 80% occupancy with half-hourly turn-over for ten hours a day to reach his sales goal. Since his products—soups, salads, and sandwiches—were in demand for only three hours a day, his goal was patently absurd. The final result? He expanded his menu, paid some much needed attention to cost control, and is still thriving, though with lowered goals.

Look at Your Profit Level

Once you have come this far, you will have three potential profit figures: one grotesquely low, one bloated—and the other, one hopes, a profit level that you and your business can live with and grow on. If the profit is not enough to cover debt retirement—which you will notice has not been covered—then you may have to stop and rethink the business from the beginning.

This is important, yet often overlooked. One of the critical financial ratios is concerned with how many times operating profit covers debt amortization, because you'll be retiring your term debt out of operating profits. And if your profit is not high enough to comfortably cover your debt repayment, you won't stay in business long. You will also be hard-put to get additional credit of any kind.

Review all expense categories, one by one. There are some expenses that will remain hidden or overlooked, no matter how careful you are. The best way to prepare for this problem is to be conservative in your projections. You will be much better off with a slightly understated profit than to plan optimistically and fail to reach your projected profit level. Basing projections on dreams rather than the real world will only hurt you and your business.

Once again, your bottom line, net profit, must be able to support your term debt and finance a major portion of your growth. If the figure is too low, be warned. (And if it is too high, that can be a danger sign, too—though it needn't be.)

Although no projection is 100% accurate, experience and review will make your forecasts more exact. Use your projection as a measure of your growth toward established objectives. Any large (or unusual) item entered on your projected profit and loss statement should be accompanied by an explanation of how you derived the figures. A simple note should suffice to remind you how the numbers were generated.

During the comparison/review process, compare your final projection to the past performance of your business. Even though the projections (both best and worst cases) have been in part based on your actual experience, it can be a shock to first review your realistic projection the middle way. Compare it, item by item, with your historical data.

Why do this? Because experience is the great corrector of projections. No matter how carefully a projection is prepared, severe divergences from past practices need additional thought. The divergence may be justifiable—but more often it reflects wishful thinking. If the projections are radically gloomy, then you should rethink them; you want your goals to be realistic, not misleading or thwarting.

Where there are significant differences between projections and past practice, make notes. Later on, they'll help you understand why you made the projections differ from past practice, an understanding which is easily lost.

Prepare a Cash Flow Projection

This step has three parts:

A. Project your monthly cash inflows.

B. Project your monthly cash disbursements (outflows).

C. Project operating data.

This will—using Figure 5.4 below—result in a realistic cash flow budget.

Cash flow depends on both dollar volume and timing. These are equally important, since cash flowing in or out of your business at the wrong time is no help at all. In the short term, avoidable cash shortages cause panic. Long term, chronic cash shortages will surely strangle the growth of your firm—or bankrupt it.

Ironically, growth is itself a major cause of cash flow problems. Not all sales are on a cash basis. You probably extend credit—and you may offer your customers more lenient terms than your suppliers offer you. Most small businesses aren't set up to pursue formal collection procedures on slow-paying accounts, so the upshot is that as you increase your sales and receivables, you run out of cash and/or trade credit.

Your cash flow budget can prevent such problems.

Or suppose that your business hits a slump—a period when even your best customers are temporarily overstocked, or don't need your services. For seasonal businesses, this can be disastrous. Reduced sales mean reduced cash inflow, while your fixed payments go on at their usual brisk clip. The result? Cash outflow exceeds inflow, and you go broke.

Whatever the cause of a cash flow problem, the result is the same: If you run out of cash, you run into trouble. Getting out of a cash flow problem may be impossible—yet in almost every case, the problem could have been avoided in the first place.

How? By preparing a cash flow budget, following it, and revising or straying from its bounds only when there are compelling reasons. The form in Figure 4 is a format we suggest for small business use. Feel free to modify it. You'll find it covers most items. Don't omit *any* details peculiar to your business, though. If (for instance) you have heavy shipping costs, make an entry for it.

A. Project Your Monthly Cash Inflows

The hardest part has already been done.

Your projected P&L for the budget period established realistic sales levels; now the task is limited to parceling those totals over the months. It is not likely that your sales are spread evenly throughout the year, with one-twelfth of the annual sales falling in each month.

Build in seasonal variations, month by month. If all of your sales are cash, enter the proceeds on the form. Ordinarily, some sales will be for cash, some for credit. Your historical records will give you the proportions and a handle on two vital items: How long does it take your average credit customer to pay? How many don't pay at all? Remember: It's not a sale until you get paid.

You can make this section as difficult as you want. However, if most of your credit customers follow 30-day terms, a credit sale in June turns into July cash. If there is a seasonal bias—for instance, if you extend credit to farmers who pay your bills when they sell their crops—then your cash flow must reflect this.

Enter the estimates for cash sales and receivables collections in the appropriate **ESTIMATE** columns. Sales are far and away the most important source of cash inflow. Many of your cost figures depend upon your sales level. If you plan to borrow funds, or generate additional equity investments, record the estimated cash inflow amounts in the appropriate months. If you plan to sell any fixed assets, the same procedure should be followed.

You probably have noticed that for cash flow purposes you ignore product line differences stressed in Part One of this topic. How come? Because your cash flow budget is concerned with cash flow more than with the sources of sales dollars. The subject is plenty complex as it stands.

WHY BUDGET?

"Income of £20.00, expenses of £19.19.6. Result: happiness. Expenses of £20.06. Result: misery." Charles Dickens was right. This is why you budget—to make sure that income exceeds outflow. Now: How do you establish a budget?

B. Project Your Monthly Cash Outflows

Once again, as you project monthly outflow let your P&L projection serve as a guide. Your fixed expenses, already identified, will remain constant every month. Rent, for example, is usually paid monthly. If it is not, spread it in the appropriate manner. Those variable expenses that remain a constant percentage of sales have also been identified; put them down as appropriate. Sales commissions, for example, are tied directly to sales. Your salespeople won't sell if they aren't paid.

Expenses that vary with sales, but not on a constant percentage basis, are the hardest expenses to enter on the form. If the relation is complex, try to find out what it is, and adjust the cash flow accordingly. If you aren't sure, be conservative. Greatly increased sales may require increased office staff, which will be reflected as an increase in fixed expenses. This is a step increase, not a smooth curve.

Remember, the "cash-paid-out" items on this form represent cash flowing out of your business, so both dollar amounts and timing are important. Most small businesses need to pay more attention to timing. Often the variations between projections and performance are not a matter of amount, but of time.

The cash outflows (and cash inflows) are recorded in the month the disbursement (or payment in cash) is actually made.

This distinction is particularly important when you are planning purchase schedules. By knowing your purchasing, sales, and sales collection cycles, you can often smooth out the peaks and valleys of your cash flow. If, for instance, you run a seasonal gift shop, you may have to incur expenses in June that will be paid in October. Your cash flow should reflect this. Otherwise, you may have a lot of cash floating about and forget that it is already committed to retiring inventory borrowings. It happens.

For some businesses, an entry such as "Reserve for Purchases" is helpful. Plan for a large annual expense, or a single payment debt service, and make sure it's budgeted.

All of your disbursements must be recorded on the cash flow/budget projection—all expenses, debt retirement, owner's withdrawals, capital purchases. Cash disbursements that don't get recorded diminish the effectiveness of your budget, so be thorough.

If you plan to expand your business or to acquire or replace equipment, enter those costs and their timing. This affords another chance for review of your plans for the budgetary period. You may find it helpful to apply the same worst/best/most likely case analysis to your proposed acquisition. Most small companies make major purchases without adequate consideration of alternatives. If you have to disburse cash, make sure it goes into a necessary purchase.

C. Project Operating Data

This is merely a continuation of the process.

First: The monthly cash flow is derived by subtracting the cash outflows from the cash inflows. If the cash flow is negative, it may be temporary and of little concern—but if your projections show a chronic negative cash flow, you have a major problem.

You can try to speed up cash flow: increase sales, try for speedier collection of receivables, slow down a bit on payables. But these are not always options.

You may be carrying too much debt, or debt of the wrong kind. If you are using short-term notes to finance acquisition of capital assets or long-term needs, then this will cause major cash flow problems. Ask your banker to review your debt structure with you. Restructuring debt can ease cash flow problems.

Once you are aware of the possible problems that lie ahead, you can do something about them. It's always the unforeseen hazard that causes the biggest problems.

Second: To convert your cash flow budget (which you have now completed) to operating P&L use, add up non-cash expenses such as depreciation and then subtract this from the total. If your company is marginal, this simple test may spotlight areas you can improve.

Review and Revise Quarterly

Review your forecast once again to determine how realistic your projections are. All operating data for the past twelve months should be available. This data helps you keep on track. If you compare your budget with past experience and with industry averages (if available), you can get a measure of how accurate it will be. Large deviations are warning flags for your use—heed them.

If you project a dramatic increase in sales, how will those sales be generated? Can you afford those sales? Will you need new people? What are the cash flow implications? Your budget should reflect these concerns clearly—and your notes, as mentioned earlier, should be an aid to rethinking your projections.

The next step in the review process takes time: Test your projections quarterly. This tends to be long enough to smooth out some of the inevitable month-to-month variations, yet short enough to ensure that no problem will be allowed to grow to disastrous proportions.

You may wish to use Rolling 3's: Each month under this review method, you review the current month and the two preceding months, comparing actual with projected figures. This affords a constant and comprehensive review. If substantial differences show up, alter the projections for the next month. Then repeat the process the following month—this tends to smooth out the inevitable month-to-month ripples, while allowing your basic budget to remain pretty much constant.

By checking three-month segments on a monthly basis, you will also find that you gain a heightened awareness of short-term trends, both in your business and the general economy. For instance, personnel turnover tends to make small businesses waver from projections. As the new personnel work into their jobs and become less demanding of the already skilled personnel, the business returns to the projected course.

So review your achievements and budgets on a monthly basis, but don't change your budget unless your review suggests a major error in your projections. A budget is designed to assist in the normal operations of your business, not in unpredictable variations which are felt for only a week or a month. Of course, you will want to note the impact of these extraordinary events—and perhaps keep a log of them. Sometimes extraordinary events, seen from a longer point of view, form a subtle pattern.

To the cash on hand at the beginning of the period, add cash inflows and subtract cash outflows. The total is your new cash position for the next month. Once more: By comparing your projections to the actual figures, you will get a handle on how well your projections and your budget are working out. If there are extreme variations, check further, although you'll be well advised to check item by item to ensure that your budget is working and being followed.

If you have a temporary cash shortage, look for the cause. Ask why that cash shortage is there—your forecast will help. A problem defined is a problem half solved.

The key to effective management is knowing what is going on, what has gone on, and where your business is heading. By planning, you avert problems. By following your budget, you render your cash flow as stable as possible, which in turn makes planning more effective.

Suppose you have a temporary cash surplus. Locate the cause. Maybe you are doing something extremely well that you hadn't planned on—or perhaps outside factors are helping you and this is a non-recurring happenstance. If you know which, you can plan and adjust accordingly. If you don't learn the cause, then you run the risk of either missing future improvements or making severe mistakes.

Cash surpluses may be generated by forgetting to pay a bill. For instance, you may have a trade payable of $1,000 for inventory that you sold for $2,000, and forgot to pay the credit. The extra $1,000 cash will have to be tracked down; otherwise it will melt away, leaving you short next month.

Don't be worried—be warned.

More likely, though, a cash surplus reflects the conservative bias of the cash flow/budgeting process, and the surplus can then be utilized to make your business more profitable. In this happy case, retire debt ahead of time. Create a cash reserve. Expand. Do whatever your business plan indicates as the best, most logical step.

Companies run on a cash flow budget are more likely to have surplus cash than companies which are not because use of a budget mandates careful monitoring of cash outflows.

What if all cash outflows are justified, yet planned cash inflow is inadequate and you suffer a net cash outflow'? Then you have no choice. You have to generate additional cash somehow or go under. With a cash flow budget at hand, this problem, while severe, is not insuperable. Since you know how much cash you need and when you need it, you have the beginnings of a financing proposal.

In fact, a well-documented cash flow budget will serve as the heart of your financing proposal if you and your business are already known to your banker. It demonstrates that you know what you're doing and that you take all due precautions. Such careful management appeals to bankers.

Why? The cash flow budgeting process shows that you care enough about the future of your business to establish goals, and that you have mapped out a route to achieve those goals. The implied discipline is impressive.

Compare Budgeted with Actual Performance Monthly

Now what?

You have aimed your business in the right direction. Your budget keeps it on track—and this is where the cash flow/budget form comes in handy.

Always determine the reason for a deviation from your budget.

You create your budget under optimal conditions. All the information you have, with time to reflect upon it, improved by review and experience, gives you a sound budget. When you deviate from it, as you will, most likely you will do so under less than ideal conditions—panic, confusion, hustle and bustle, constant interruptions.

Decisions made under stress are seldom as fruitful as those made under conditions more conducive to clear thought. So, when a major deviation is forced upon you, jot it down. Keep a notebook to record your reasons, your response, and whether what you did was right or wrong. This will help when you prepare the next version of your budget, and will also make you think twice before blowing it up.

Do this faithfully and it pays off. You'll develop:

• an excellent source of current information;

• an accurate test of the projections you have prepared;

• a fix on trends, both good and bad, affecting your business.

Most importantly, your budget will reduce the uncertainties inherent in business decision-making and allow you to make the best decisions for your business.

For instance, your budget can alert you to the need to hire more employees if you need a higher level of output to survive, and tell you when to hire them. It can tell you what expansion will do to your cash position, both now and over the long run. It can help you pin down timing on major capital expenditures so you won't have to purchase major items before you are ready. You'll be protected against impulsive commitment of funds. By scrutinizing major deals—as your budget compels—you may spot flaws beforehand, or new and more exciting applications. Budgeting works for you either way.

Review Performance

In any event, first project your sales, then your expenses, for the budgeting period. Then, using the insights and information of your P&L forecast, push a monthly cash flow, listing your projected cash inflows and outflows in the columns headed ESTIMATE. In the columns headed ACTUAL, record the actual amounts, line by line, on a monthly basis. This affords a chance to spot trends and deviations early—so they can be understood, managed and utilized.

Finally, review and revise your forecast/cash flow budget as necessary. Try to keep your balance on revisions. If you frequently tinker with your budget, it won't help you maintain direction. On the other hand, a budget shouldn't be a straitjacket; if you have sufficient reason to change your budget, change it.

Frederick Adler, a famous venture capitalist in New York, had T-shirts made up that stated "Happiness is Positive Cash Flow." Your Cash Flow Budget will result in positive cash flow—and some measure of commercial happiness.

Figure 5.4

Cash Flow Projection Chart, 19—

Use Whole Dollars	$ Estimate	%	$ Actual	%
1. Cash on Hand (beginning of month)				
2. Cash Receipts				
(a) Cash Sales				
(b) Collections from Credit Accounts,				
(c) Loan or Other Cash Injection (Specify)				
3. Total Cash Receipts (2a>+2b>+2c=>3)				
4. Total Cash Available				
(Before cash out) (1 + 3)				
5. Cash Paid Out				
Purchases (Merchandise)				
Business Taxes, Licenses				
Employer's share Social Security				
Unemployment				
Rent				
Repairs and Maintenance				
Gross Salaries				
Insurance				
Professional Fees				
Commissions				
Interest and Bank Charges				
Advertising				
Auto—Truck				

Dues and Subscriptions		
Office Supplies		
Telephone		
Utilities		
Operating Supplies		
Travel		
Laundry and Uniform		
Entertainment		
Contract Services		
Miscellaneous		
Subtotal		
Loan Principal Payment		
Capital Purchases (Specify)		
Other Start-up Costs		
Owner's Withdrawal		
6. Total Cash Paid Out		
7. Cash Position		
(End of month) (4 minus 6)		
Essential Operating Data		
A. Non—Cash Flow Information		
Sales Volume (Dollars)		
B. Accounts Receivable (End of month)		
C. Bad Debts (End of month)		
D. Inventory on Hand (End of month)		
E. Accounts Payable (End of month)		
F. Depreciation		

Action Plan For:
Forecasting and Cash Flow Budgeting

☐ Set business guidelines and goals.

☐ Review current economic and business conditions; consider how they will affect your business.

☐ Forecast sales for the budget period.

☐ Forecast expenses for the budget period.

☐ Prepare a Profit & Loss projection.

☐ Run a reality check on the numbers. Compare them to your goals, trade figures, historical figures.

☐ Project monthly cash inflows for the budget period.

☐ Project monthly cash disbursements (outflows) for the budget period.

☐ Project operating data. Move controllable items about to achieve the best positive cash flow possible.

☐ Prepare your Cash Flow Budget: the "finished" Cash Flow Projection. Look for periods of negative cash flow; look for unusually positive periods also.

☐ Compare Budgeted with Actual Performance Monthly.

☐ Review Performance and recast forecasts (both P&L and Cash Flow) annually or as needed.

Chapter Six:

Cash Flow Management

....

You can't look at your cash flow from too many angles. Nor can you look at the financial composition of your business too carefully; knowing how to manage your cash flow (and hence financing) makes the difference between succeeding brilliantly and failing dismally.

Cash flow spells survival for every business. Manage cash flow effectively, and your business works. Costs are in order. Sales and collection efforts work together, margins are protected, market share is growing, and all is right with your commercial world.

If your cash flow is not well managed, then sooner or later your business goes under.

It's that simple. A positive cash flow is one where cash comes in faster than it goes out. Maintain this—which includes paying your bills on time as well as making investments in growth—and a lot of other business problems melt. If you need more capital or more debt in order to grow, you can get it on reasonable terms. You can try out new ideas, products, markets.

The corollary is that if cash flow is mismanaged, you can't do much more than struggle to stay afloat.

Most businesses are somewhere in between these two poles. They have a positive cash flow and meet their bills, earn a modest profit, and can afford to seek new business. And sometimes—more often than they like—they find themselves suffering from a negative cash flow. On balance, they should end up in the black—but there can be some grim times in the middle.

Figure 6.1

**Five Severe Warning Signs of
Cash Flow Problems**

1. Decreased Liquidity: running out of working capital.
2. Overtrading: turning inventories faster than trade averages.
3. Excessive Short-Term Debt.
4. Missing Discounts: payables over terms.
5. Slow Collections: outstanding receivables piling up if you suffer from any of these, you have a cash flow problem.

The nut, monthly fixed expenses which must be paid on a regular basis—that is, their schedules can't be tampered with—is the silent strangler of cash flow.

What causes cash flow blues? We find three major causes: the nut gets imperceptibly bigger, a few costs slip out of control; some sales don't turn into cash on time. There are others—but these are the big ones.

This chapter outlines the steps to take to improve a less than optimal cash flow performance. The steps aren't magical or mysterious or even new.

But they work.

Some of them are painful. Cutting the nut can be difficult. Giving up a future profit (perhaps illusory) in order to preserve the business can be painful. When you're singing the cash flow blues, the present may seem grim, but expectations for the future may seem pretty alluring.

Most of the steps look simpler than they are. Stick with them. Cash flow problems are caused by the slow accretion of small expenditures over a long time.

You may feel that running a business according to a tight-fisted budget is dull. Consider the alternative, though: not running your own business at all because it has gone bust.

Manage for Survival

The first aim of any business is to remain in business. All decisions should be made with this in mind.

Cash flow difficulties kill more small businesses than any other cause. This is partly due to the thin capitalization such businesses ordinarily have, but is also due to the subtle, insidious nature of cash flow problems.

Cash flow problems sneak up on you. A major calamity—such as the failure of a major supplier which in turn causes the loss of several month's sales—is the exception. More often, cash flow trouble is the aggregate result of many tiny errors.

Consider the case of the company that, in anticipation of a major new piece of business, hired extra people, moved to a larger, more expensive location, took on some new equipment, spent a lot of selling time in negotiations with the other parties to the contract, and ended up in a cash bind. To solve the cash bind, they took on new short-term debt—and then the first payment under the contract was put off for six months.

The result? They joined the legion singing the cash flow blues.

All of the moves they made were—up to a point—sensible. When any business embarks on a period of sharp growth, some cash flow lag is inevitable. More fixed assets will be needed. New personnel (with the implied training costs) will be needed. More working capital is required to float the higher levels of inventory and receivables.

But it all hinges on getting paid—what amounts, and when.

What can be done to avoid a similar cash crunch in the future?

Keep the business' survival in mind first. By first securing the contract—and making sure of the payment schedule—you improve cash flow and ensure that the business survives even if negotiations hit a snag.

The best cash flow management policy is based on keeping the business solvent—that is, always able to meet current obligations. Any other policy takes too great a risk; all too often, hindsight shows that cash was expended needlessly, and on long shots or frivolities.

Many businesses learn this lesson the hard way. They fear that if they don't gear up, they won't get the business, yet if they gear up prematurely, they come close to disaster.

Keep the prime aim—survival—in focus at all times. If gearing up could lead to disaster, you can't afford to. If hiring a person now, instead of waiting until you need that person, won't make your business better, don't hire now.

Most simply put, expenditures you don't incur won't hurt your cash flow.

List Cash Inflows

There are only four sources of cash:

1. **Operating profits**
2. **Sale of fixed assets**
3. **New investment**
4. **New debt**

That's all. Of the four, operating profits are far and away the most important.

The other three sources are at best sporadic. At times, the sale (and sometimes the leaseback) of fixed assets is the best source of cash. New investment from you may be the only way to keep your business going. At times new debt makes the most sense.

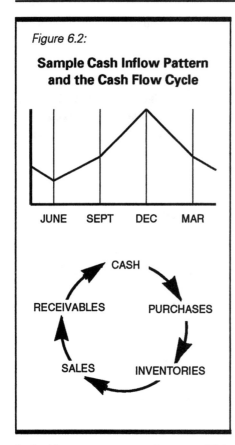

Figure 6.2:

Sample Cash Inflow Pattern and the Cash Flow Cycle

JUNE SEPT DEC MAR

CASH

RECEIVABLES PURCHASES

SALES INVENTORIES

In the long run if your business doesn't take in more cash than it has to lay out you won't have a business any longer.

This is so obvious that we almost hate to mention it Occasionally, we all lose sight of the importance of operating profitability. If you don't produce operating profits, or can't show where they will come from very soon, then no one in his or her right mind would invest or lend money to you. Many large companies are somewhat different: Chrysler and Lockheed, for example, continued to get new debt money even while suffering losses.

Small businesses do not have such latitude. If they don't make a cash flow profit on operations, they go under.

Managing for cash flow is managing for survival.

To manage your cash flow, start by looking at your past performance. Unless you have good reasons to expect differently, your business will repeat the same general patterns year after year.

For example, one business is tied to a limited number of large customers. While the number of customers is growing, their basic profile remains the same. This company confidently expects to do more than 80% of their dollar sales volume between October and March, with much of the cash coming in in January, due to the budget cycles of their largest customers. They don't anticipate any changes in this pattern, and have taken the cash flow implications into their planning efforts.

Your business has a definite cash flow cycle. Look for it. Start by listing the cash inflows on a calendar (or on 3 by 5 cards), paying particular attention to when the cash comes in. Creating a receivable is one thing—getting the cash in is another, and more important for most businesses. A huge uncollected receivable is a major source of the cash flow blues. Should you need the money for the rent, that unpaid invoice won't satisfy the landlord.

You may wish to separate the inflows into the four basic categories: Operating Profits, Sale of Fixed Assets, New Investment, and New Debt. Unless your business is based on unusual financing, make sure that you treat the last three as one-time events.

An exception: seasonal borrowing is such a part of most retail companies' plans that from one year to the next, there will be little alteration in the amount and timing of the cash inflow from that kind of borrowing. Use your own judgment here: if you have this debt pattern, include it in your plans.

That leaves operating profits. You have to start with this—every variable expense (expense depending on sales volume) depends on it.

On a month-by-month basis, set down what you expect to receive in actual cash next year. This requires that you know when your customers pay their bills. If you extend credit, you should know from experience. If you are new to the game, ask more experienced players like your banker.

To be conservative, don't expect your customers to continue to pay on time (if indeed they have been paying promptly). Expect their performance to slide. Many companies look for about 15 to 30 days beyond terms.

If you get a few large orders out of the blue now and again, do not try to count on them to balance your cash flow. It's better by far to be pleasantly surprised. The cost of not getting an order because you weren't prepared for it is far lower than being well prepared for an order that never arrives.

List Cash Outflows

You have unlimited numbers of ways to dribble away cash: payroll, inventory, travel, supplies, advertising, space costs, taxes and so on.

Start by reviewing last year's budget against last year's disbursement performance.

If you don't have a budget, drop everything until you and your accountant can get together. (Or follow the directions in Chapter Five.)

Then immediately begin to put a cash flow budget together. It is the single most important task to ensure the survival of your business.

What is the upside potential of not using a budget? Cheap thrills? Or saving a few hours of careful work on the budget, including periodically reviewing how well the budget works for you'? The downside risk is clear enough, but we've yet to see any advantage in refusing to control costs.

Look to your budget. The expenses may be constant, but the cash disbursements won't be. For example, suppose your insurance costs $1,200 per year. For an accrual budget, that works out to be $100 per month. (The expense is incurred in equal amounts.) On a cash flow budget, however, the cost might be $100 per month, or $1,200 in March, or $300 a quarter, if that's the payment schedule.

Timing is as important as the dollar amount when you consider cash flow.

Determine when payment has to be made in cash. You want to keep track of when the obligation is incurred, but what matters here is the actual cash disbursement You might be more comfortable with a $1,200 payment in March than a $300 payment in August; it is a function of *your* cash flow.

For most businesses, cash journals and checkbooks provide the specific historical information on just when you paid bills. If you have been managing for cash flow, this is an easy step. If you have not, it becomes a bit more tricky. The disbursements were probably made sporadically, their timing more dependent on when you had cash available than on when it would be best (from a cash flow standpoint) to pay the bills.

Now list on the same calendars or other sheets you used for the prospective inflows, when you expect to be making specific cash disbursements. These will fall into two main groups: fixed and variable.

Fixed monthly disbursements—as examples, office and administrative payroll, insurance, utilities and basic telephone, interest on principal payments on term loans, rent or mortgage—present a special problem.

A normal increase in the nut is understandable if not inevitable. The cost of everything rises because inflation pushes it up. Salaries go up; otherwise you lose your best people. Supplies go up. Maintenance and utility costs go up. Energy costs aggravate it and so it goes.

Your task is to make a serious effort never to add unnecessarily to the nut. Those single costs appear innocuous, but on a yearly basis, they become pretty scary.

Figure 6.3

Cash Flow Analysis Form

June

INFLOWS		OUTFLOWS	
		Disbursement:	
Source	**Amount**	**Fixed**	**Amount**
Customer A	$4800	Rent	$725
Customer B	1250	Loan payment	1200
		Disbursement: Variable	
		Printer	$675
		Sales commission	480
TOTAL:_____		TOTAL:_____	

Again, creeping costs make the nut a problem. It's like the death by a thousand cuts: each increment whittles you down.

Kept low, your nut represents the necessary costs of doing business. Not checked against a budget, it will choke your business—like many people, you'll be left wondering why that large increase in sales never got to the bottom line. And why you suddenly ran out of cash. The response to this kind of problem is frequently to borrow a little more for working capital, on a term basis. This merely drives the nut up further, compounding the problem and making it even more difficult to earn an operating profit.

Variable costs are tricky also. If you face a period of sharp growth, the costs specifically associated with that growth tend to shoot up faster than receipts turn to cash, and the result is strangulation of the cash flow. To prevent this you will probably need financing; it is extremely unusual to be able to finance fast growth out of your operating profits.

If you expect next year to be much like this one, then your variable costs

Figure 6.4

"We thought we needed a copying machine. Before we got one though, we analyzed our needs with some caution, taking note of the number of copies we needed to make each day for a month.

"We discovered, somewhat to our surprise, that we could drop the work off daily (one of us would go to the copy store down the street at lunch or on a coffee break) and the total cost was about $30 per month. In order to purchase or lease a copier for our realistic workload, we'd have to pay $50 per month, and still take big orders to the copy store. Supplies added another $10, so we'd be paying about $60 per month for the same work— that we could do for $30 (plus, admittedly, some inconvenience).

"Still, $1 a day difference is not much. What if, we asked, we had a lot more work? Wouldn't it make sense to be prepared?

"That's how the nut creeps up. The cost looks small and can be argued into insignificance.

"We decided to put up with the inconvenience until the cost made sense. And a client told us that costs would go up faster— a copier invites use for recipes, cartoons, articles for friends and so on. That extra $30 or so each month becomes $360 or more per year— and costs like that add up."

—A small business owner.

will follow the same pattern. In such a case, make your projections accordingly. If you do anticipate a major shift in how you do business, then seek the help of your accountant.

Look for Cash Flow Trends

Much of the difficulty of management lies in details. In the heat of day-to-day operations, you can lose sight of important trends. If you practice deviation analysis, a formal method of comparing actual against budgeted performance on a monthly and on a year-to-date basis, you won't miss many cash flow danger signals.

Figure 6.5

**Establish a Plan for
Positive Cash Flow**

1. Put down the cash flow items which cannot be changed to other dates.
2. List anticipated cash inflows, allowing a margin for safety—if your receivables average 30 days, use 45 days for planning.
3. Then allocate payment dates to suit your needs—don't forget to take full advantage of trade credit, but do NOT abuse it.

What if you still have shortfalls?

You should congratulate yourself for being realistic. This shortfall indicates need for some kind of financing.

At the very least you should sit down monthly and try to discern whether cash income is on target with projections and whether the nut is being held in check. Major cash outlays usually get accorded a lot of thought; minor ones do not, and businesses suffer as a result

Examine Timing

If cash inflow lags behind outflow, you have a problem, one you should address immediately.

On the other hand, if cash inflow is ahead of outflow, then you may have the happy discovery of idle cash—money you can put to another use, such as fueling growth, retiring debt and lowering the nut, trying out a new market, or making a new product.

On a large calendar, match up (by week or by month) cash inflows and outflows. Many successful businesses do this on a daily basis, which may seem extreme, though it is hard to quibble with success.

Sum up both inflows and outflows. Are they changing? Keep year-to-date as well as monthly records to smooth out temporary aberrations and to spotlight really subtle trends which develop over a period of months.

It's obvious that there's an incipient problem if cash disbursements are being made later and later each month, or if a major customer cancels that large order which you had slotted to provide 85% of the May cash flow. (Incidentally, concentrating your business in a few accounts may be risky. For survival, you do better to have 100 customers paying $1,000 apiece than one who pays $100,000—the chances are slight that you would lose 100 customers at one time.)

But the obvious dramas rarely put a business in a hopeless position. The really dangerous problem is the one you don't see until it's almost too late—a characteristic of cash flow problems.

Control Cash Outflows

The natural urge, when hit by a big cash flow problem, is to try to build up sales while paring expenses.

That's fine, but all too often the wrong costs are cut and the least likely customers pursued.

Your quickest return will usually come from cutting the nut.

How? By rescheduling payments, you can almost always gain several weeks grace without losing the respect of your suppliers and creditors. Your banker, for example, would much prefer that you ask to make interest-only payments to ease you through a cash crunch than have you skip payments without any explanation at all. If you took your banker's advice in good times (when the loan was made) you should take it in bad times as well. Take it now, from an expert, when the cash flow is tight.

You can't tamper with fixed payments that are legally tied to a schedule. You cannot shift paydays about on whim, but other payments are often movable, and to your benefit.

To "lean on trade" (stall payment without explanation until your creditors put lighted matches under your toes) is often recommended by the irresponsible. This is an utterly foolish way to deal with a cash flow problem, and you can only make enemies.

If you cannot make a payment on time, don't compound the problem. Your creditors know when you miss a payment. To say, "The check is in the mail" or to send an empty envelope or an unsigned check or pull any of the thousands of other stunts won't help you either. They will make your creditors angry, and angry creditors will either pull the plug or put you on a cash-only basis.

Call your creditors. Explain the problem. explain how you plan to handle it and perhaps offer to make partial payments until things turn around. You will probably be given a chance to breathe.

Put yourself in their shoes: if one of your customers asked for a reduced payment plan because of a cash crunch, while another refused to return your calls and letters, which one would you carry?

Another possible source of relief is to refinance debt. It takes longer than rescheduling monthly payments, and may be either expensive or impossible. However: if you have a monthly debt payment of $1,000, it may be better to refinance at $700 a month even if the interest rate is substantially higher. Your nut will be lower, a help to a major cash flow crisis. As your cash position improves, you might then be able to reduce the principal—but that's another kind of cash flow device.

Rescheduling works. Refinancing works. And reducing the nut always helps.

Your aim throughout is to match up inflows and outflows, with the outflows always following the inflows. If you can arrange to do this without cutting yourself off from the possibility of growing (hyper-conservatism doesn't pay a big dividend in growth), you won't be sorry.

Summary

If you manage your business for cash flow, you accomplish several benefits:

1. You will have your attention firmly riveted on generating and maintaining operating profits.

2. You will be compelled to work within the bounds of a budget geared to your own cash flow needs; this prevents careless errors that cut profitability.

3. You will find that you can grow—and secure the necessary financing to do so with minimal risk.

Action Plan For:
Cash Flow Management

☐ Manage for survival. You can't make a profit if you aren't in business.

☐ List cash inflows from all sources, by amount and date. Summarize to keep it manageable.

☐ Study and understand your cash flow cycle. Each business has its own patterns.

☐ List cash outflows. What patterns do they display? Which can be jiggled about to ease cash flow squeezes?

☐ Look for long-term cash flow trends.

☐ Control cash outflows by using your cash flow budget. Check performance monthly against budget.

Chapter Seven:

Debt Management and Financing

....

Managing cash flow in order to maintain enough liquidity to meet current obligations and take advantage of opportunities guarantees survival.

Cash flow management leads to debt management. What levels of debt can your business safely support? Can you control the amount, timing, and availability of credit? That is, can you ensure the timely inflow of cash from new debt?

Assume that you have done all you can realistically do to control your cash flow, but you still face occasional periods of cash shortfalls. To tide you over these periods, you have to borrow from a commercial bank. How do you go about preparing a financing proposal?

This chapter is intended to help you understand and deal with your banker as an equal. It augments the earlier chapter on financing. Its five steps follow from the basic cash flow controls, unless your cash flow is already under control additional financing is unwise.

Focus on Receivables, Credit, Collection and Inventory

Your largest current assets are probably receivables and inventory.

Ideally, both of these assets turn into cash as soon as you wish. However, unless you manage them carefully, they tend to become a problem. To manage your working capital properly, you must know:

> *Figure 7.1*
>
> ### Five Steps in Receivables Management
>
> 1. Age your receivables.
>
> 2. Calculate your collection period and apply the rule of thumb to see if you have a receivables problem.
>
> 3. Identify the slow-paying customers.
>
> 4. Pursue delinquent accounts vigorously.
>
> 5. Identify fast-pay accounts and try to increase their number.

1. The age of your receivables and inventory;

2. The turn of your receivables and inventory;

3. The concentration of your receivables (how many customers, what amount of receivables they represent, what products the receivables cover) and the concentration of inventory by product lines.

You must also know what your credit and collection policies are doing to your working capital. All too often small business owners mistake sales for profits. They extend more and more credit, pursue lax collection policies, and end up financing their customers in order to increase sales. One business owner (and he's not alone) found that his largest accounts actually cost him money because of slow payment.

No one can afford to provide interest-free loans to their bulk customers, but until you take time to analyze the payment practices of your slow paying accounts, you may not know who's eating up profits.

This isn't to say that credit sales should not increase. But the aim is *profitability*, not just sales increases. If the sales increases don't translate into profits on the bottom line, then you are buying trouble faster than you are buying sales.

Receivables Management

To control receivables, begin by examining their age. Break receivables out weekly to spot the slow-pay accounts as soon as possible. Then you can try to collect before the accounts cost you your profits.

> *Figure 7.2*
>
> ### Three Credit Policy Steps
>
> 1. Divide your customer list into three groups: Prime, Good, Other. Prime customers always pay within term; Good usually do; Others seldom if ever do.
>
> 2. Look for similarities within the groups: What kinds of customers are apt to be Prime or Good? How are they different from Other?
>
> 3. Look for ways to upgrade as many customers as possible to Prime and Good. Remember: You don't have a sale until you're paid.

Aging receivables is simple: Separate invoices into Current, 30 days, 60 days, 90 days and over. Depending on your particular needs, you may wish to do this more tightly.

Then, figure out your collection period: Divide annual credit sales by 360 to find the average daily credit sale. Next, divide your current outstanding receivables total by the average daily credit sale, this yields your collection period.

A good rule of thumb to heed: If your collection period is more than one third greater than your credit terms (for example, 40 days if your terms are Net 30), you have a credit and collection problem that needs attention.

Credit and Collection

The cost of extending credit is one of those hidden costs that eats up working capital. Most of us aren't credit experts; we grant credit terms because others do, and fail to understand what we are doing, Very few smaller businesses have explicit credit policies. If they did, they could dramatically increase both profits and the quality of their current assets.

You should investigate the possible use of credit cards. These cost little in return for the headaches they save you. Consider the cost, in direct bad debt losses, and in time, effort and attention that slow-pay accounts cost you. The added costs of capital tied up in receivables, for example, is frequently greater than the discount charged by the major credit card companies.

Figure 7.3

Collections

Name: _____

Telephone: _____

Spoke To: _____

Title: _____

Subject: _____

Date: _____

Time: _____

Initials: _____

☐ No Answer   ☐ Not Available

☐ Requested Info   ☐ Requested Proof of Delivery

☐ Order Never Received   ☐ Payment Previously Sent

☐ Will Send Check   ☐ Merchandise Returned

☐ Duplicate Billing   ☐ Payment Being Held

Comments:_____

Returned Call:_____

Follow-up:_____

_____

Use the form in Figure 7.3 every time you call a lagging account. It provides back-up information if you turn the account over to a collection agency or have to prosecute the matter in court. The completed slip should be filed for reference on further calls. The form provides a structure for the calls themselves.

Remember to ask for **specific payments on specific dates**. If payment is not received, call back and ask again.

Inventory

Inventory management, like receivables management, is often overlooked as a source of operating profits. Careful attention to how you manage these two areas can often spring cash and improve operating profits without recourse to bank borrowing. If you are managing both of these areas well, congratulate yourself—you are in a distinct minority.

Carrying costs of inventory can run as high as 30% of average inventory, a substantial drain on working capital. Consider the costs of storage, spoilage, pilferage, inventory loans and so on. They add up fast.

Determining the right level of inventory to carry is a difficult problem. On the one hand you want to avoid unnecessary expenses, while on the other you want to avoid as many stockouts as possible. Trying to manage inventory on a day-to-day basis invites trouble; accordingly, most businesses use some kind of inventory policy.

The three most important factors in deciding on an inventory policy are *inventory turn* (how many times per year, and how does that compare with other businesses in the same line?), *reorder time* (planning on a ten day reorder time is vastly different from a 210 day reorder), and who your *suppliers* are.

Lack of inventory control is a silly risk to run. If your inventory gets too high, you run out of cash. If it is too low, the chances are excellent that either you are buying in uneconomical quantities (a danger sign to bankers), are too undercapitalized to ever become profitable (another danger sign), or are bleeding the business. Bankers are increasingly interested in the quality of inventory as well as the more standard indicators of good management (liquidity, profitability, and track record). If you have a cogent inventory policy, and follow it, you will upgrade both inventory quality and profitability.

Figure 7.4

Some Basic Inventory Considerations

1. Inventory cost and mix.
2. Carrying costs.
3. Economical ordering quantities (EOQ).
4. Stockout policies.
5. Bargain policies—BEWARE.
6. Replacement, availability, and reorder times.

Establish a Contingency Plan

A contingency plan is a plan you hope never to use: it outlines what you would do if all of your optimistic plans went wrong.

It doesn't have to be lengthy. In some cases, it can be as short as a single page and still be more than adequate, although for most businesses it will be somewhat longer.

A contingency plan should provide answers to the following questions:

1. What suppliers would give you extended terms or carry you—in case of a crunch? Why would they carry you? How long, and how much?

2. What new investment could you make? Would you refinance personal assets to provide a cash cushion for your business? Could you? What other assets could you bring to support a cash crunch?

3. What assets does your business have to either sell or turn to cash (perhaps a sale/leaseback) some other way if necessary?

4. How will you keep your banker and major trade creditors on your side?

5. Have you examined all possible sources of additional working capital in your business? Where might you have some leverage?

6. What customers would be willing to prepay or speed up orders if it would help you?

The purpose of a contingency plan is to make sure before a crisis is at hand that you won't panic. As evidence of thoughtful business management, it's hard to beat, and is being sought by more and more creditors.

Incidentally, the purpose of collateralizing a loan (for small business, this usually means pledging personal assets to support a business loan) is not to make the bank a second-hand asset dealer but to tie you more closely to the business. If all the assets at stake belong to the bank, and times get tough, you might be tempted to let go sooner than if your own assets were at stake.

Tighten and Maintain Cash Controls

Cash flow control begins with the cash flow budget. If you don't have a cash flow budget, you will have cash flow problems.

You also need a sales budget or its equivalent to keep the sales level where it should be. Small sales lags can add up to big problems if not spotted early—ranging from a less than honest clerk to a sluggish salesperson.

Your cash flow budget is a tool for keeping overhead costs down. You have a degree of control over costs that you don't have over sales; while you can almost always cut costs, you can't generate sales (especially cash sales) whenever you need to. If you could, you'd never have a cash flow problem and would not need financing.

Every budget has some fat in it. Tightening controls means always asking whether this or that purchase or expenditure will have a positive effect on your business. If there is no clear answer, the expenditure should be closely examined.

This cannot be a now and then effort. To work, it must be consistent. All the controls in the book will do you no good unless they are applied—whether the control is a separation of purchasing from paying, making sure that bills and reorders go out when they should, or even keeping a physical count of the inventory.

This is particularly true of your budget. Many businesses have budgets that are models of accountancy, but if the budget is not used, it is useless. It can be a sharp and painful lesson that does not bear repeating.

Tighten your controls. Then apply them—and monitor for results.

Determine Your Financing Needs

At some point, no matter how carefully you monitor your cash flow, you will have to borrow money from a commercial bank. There are two main reasons to borrow: to cover a temporary cash flow gap, and to provide working capital for growth. Many small businesses, however, use financing mainly to hide the effects of operating losses.

Plan ahead. A written financing plan—whether for bank or internal use—is a major step in the right direction. A financing plan helps you to avoid cash flow problems, anticipate financing needs (for growth or for survival), and helps keep your total borrowing under control.

A financing plan spells out detailed responses to such questions as: What are the needs? Why can't they be met from retained earnings? Are operating profits going to be available to meet long-term debt? How much is needed, when, and under what terms?

Most importantly, the plan should provide an answer to the banker's biggest question: How will this loan be repaid?

You must be able to show that you can afford to service the loan. One of the classic ways small businesses trip themselves up is to use this year's financing to pay off last year's debt. This pyramiding is doubly defeating. It creates a larger debt load than is wise, and it is very discouraging to be always behind the eight-ball even while the profitability is going up. Be wary of using financing to conceal operating losses.

How do you put together a financing plan? Start by identifying the different needs for funds. Most of these will be covered by operating profits. Those that cannot be (or cannot without making the liquidity vanish) should be carefully analyzed to see whether more debt should be sought.

The important thing to keep in mind is that if debt financing is needed to cover a cash flow gap ordinarily caused by insufficient operating profits, the underlying cause must be identified and dealt with before financing will do any good. Borrowing to paper over an operating problem always leads to a worsened situation, tempting though it may be at the time.

Figure 7.5

Five Financing Plan Steps

1. Clearly identify the need for loan funds.

2. Determine the amounts you need.

3. Determine the timing of your needs: short-term, long-term, or other, as well as the date of disbursement you want.

4. What kind of financing is most appropriate for your business? Why?

5. How will the money be repaid? Document with cash flows, projected profit and loss statements, and balance sheets.

Suppose, for example, that your sales have fallen off and costs have risen, making it clear that soon you will have a severe liquidity or working capital problem. If the lag in sales can be cured without borrowing, fine. (You can, as pointed out repeatedly, almost always take costs down a few notches.) If you will still have a cash flow problem, then make sure that the borrowing won't make it worse. If the sales problem can't be resolved, sooner or later you'll be back to the bank to borrow more, thus driving costs even higher.

Make sure you know your needs before going to the bank—both in dollar terms and in what benefits that cash inflow will have. Any banker you'd want to work with will ask—almost before you sit down, what you need the money for and whether you could raise it from operations. To stammer and admit you haven't looked for operating economies and profits as a way to generate money is a sure way to lose credibility.

Avoid this. Enter the bank well prepared.

Legitimate financing needs fall into five related categories. At any one time you may need to use several of these. A startup, for example, may be read as including radical expansion, perhaps by acquisition or by starting up a brand new division.

1. Startups: A new business needs a combination of investment capital and long-term debt. One error that cripples a lot of small businesses is the use of short-term debt to finance long-term needs. The basic rule in financing is to match the term of the loan to both the term of the need and to the source of repayment. Using a 90-day note for permanent financing needs is very risky. Not only is there the ever-present danger that the loan will not be renewed (bank examiners frown on "ever-green" notes), but there is the added disadvantage of never being able to plan more than 90 days ahead.

2. Working capital shortages: After initial capitalization, working capital should be generated from operating profits, over a long period. If you suffer from chronic working capital shortages due to under-capitalization, but are making some operating profits, then the answer may be a term loan if you can demonstrate that the loan will more than repay itself in additional operating profits. Sometimes a modest working capital loan will put a business over the hump, affording enough breathing room to make much higher operating profits.

But remember: A working capital loan, which is paid back monthly over a period of three to seven years, adds to the basic nut. If your business won't generate sufficient operating profits to cover the payments comfortably, then added equity is needed, not another loan.

3. Equipment and other fixed assets: Equipment and other fixed asset loans are about the clearest example of matching a loan to the need and repayment base. Since these loans are ordinarily secured by the equipment, the anticipated useful life of the equipment becomes a major factor in the credit decision.

A very rough guideline is that you can finance equipment with a projected useful life of ten years for up to 70% of its life, and for as much as 90% of its value.

Don't buy fixed assets on 90-day notes. The timing is wrong. If you are trying to make your business work on sweat equity, you may want to go ahead and pay off a piece of equipment more rapidly than we'd recommend. That's an option, but a hard one to live with.

While equipment loans rarely go beyond seven years, commercial real estate may be financed over ten or more years, depending on the situation. Since you are building equity in equipment and real estate over a number of years, from profits, you want to finance it in the same way.

4. Inventory; seasonal progress: These loans are short-term, and usually are tied to a clearly defined source of repayment such as one inventory turn, fulfillment of a contract, or sale of a specific asset.

Short-term notes are repaid from short-term sources, clearly identified before the credit is granted.

Medium and long-term debts, on the other hand, are repaid from more indirect sources. A banker looks to proven management ability (usually evidenced by a profitable history and clearly understood plans) for repayment. Since there is no one fast source of repayment, the risk is greater, and the decision more difficult.

This is a crucial distinction. A poorly run company may be an excellent short-term credit risk, but for long-term credit, a business must demonstrate ability to consistently generate profits.

Remember, term loans come due every month, adding to the nut. As the nut rises, so does the risk and the need for more careful management. Your banker knows this.

5. Sustained growth: The final major category of bankable loans is for growth, which can out-strip working capital. A business anticipating fast growth can also anticipate a lot of danger. As sales go up, liquidity goes down, creating a heightened threat of insolvency. A combination of investment, lines of credit tied to receivables and inventory, and long-term working capital loans is the normal answer.

Notice what this implies. If you plan to grow, you must plan to generate profits consistently, at the same time keeping your business liquid to meet current obligations.

To make sure that you maintain liquidity, you have to make sure of your financing. The answer? A financing plan.

If your banker won't visit your place of business, you aren't getting the treatment you deserve.

Work With Your Banker

If you aren't comfortable preparing a financing proposal, complete with financial statements of all kinds, or if you feel that your banking relationships could be improved, get your banker involved in your long-term planning efforts.

Bankers are like everyone else—they like to use their skills. Since most businesses suffer from a lack of financial management skills, and since most bankers have these skills, it is to your advantage to make the first move. Invite your banker to help you.

Level with him or her. If you can't keep communications open, then you won't get help—and you will quite possibly not get the financing you need. Your banker can tell if your business is in a bind. Banks are primarily information clearinghouses, and it takes little skill to recognize altered payment and supplier relations from daily and weekly bank activities.

The sooner you can get your banker on your side, the better. If your banker won't visit your place of business, you aren't getting the treatment you deserve— after all nobody is smart enough to understand a business without actually seeing it in operation.

Summary

Debt management and cash flow management are inseparable. A poorly managed cash flow will eventually surface as a depletion of working capital. If working capital never presented a problem, you'd never have to go into debt.

Your aim is to manage cash flow to minimize debt load—and generate better profits. The right debt at the right time, under the right terms, is a powerful tool. But like any mismanaged tool, it will cause damage in direct proportion to its power.

After making sure your cash flow is under control—including receivables and inventory management—you should consider getting your banker involved in your planning. At the very least, you'll enhance your credibility; more likely, you'll find that you can turn the banker's skills into a positive resource rather than a roadblock.

Action Plan For:
Debt Management & Financing

☐ Focus on Receivables, Credit, Collection and Inventory. These can lead to an increase in cash over a short time, lessening the need to borrow.

☐ Establish a Contingency Plan. It prevents panic and builds valuable credibility.

☐ Tighten and Maintain Cash Controls—continuously.

☐ Determine your Financing Needs. Try to minimize borrowing needs whenever possible.

☐ Work with your Banker in foul times as well as fair. Check in at least quarterly.

Chapter Eight:

Financial Controls

....

In most small and growing companies, the two most important financial controls regulate costs and liquidity. These are the cash flow budget and the projected income statement. Use of these controls presupposes that you have adequate record-keeping and accounting systems. If you do not (or suspect that you do not), then review them immediately, and if necessary, replace these systems.

Without clean information, you are taking unnecessary risks.

Let's assume that you have effective accounting and bookkeeping systems which at the very least provide:

1. monthly income statements;

2. quarterly cash flow projections;

3. annual income statement and balance sheet;

4. projections—income statement balance sheet and cash flow;

5. budgets for operations and capital expenditures.

In a stable business, sales are largely predictable. Budgets can be based on extrapolations from prior years' experience. For a growing business, the problems are more complex.

First, growing companies commonly face severe cash flow problems. As sales go up, so do receivables. While your business may be showing excellent profits, you may find that your bank balance has vanished: You're in the midst of a liquidity crisis. Higher sales levels tend to drive fixed costs up in disproportionate steps. Often the company cannot afford to undertake new sales without acquiring new debt (expensive) or selling equity in the business (unpalatable).

Second, if a company grows rapidly, it overworks its capital. Consequently its financial ratios (which are indicators to bankers and other financing sources) fail to meet criteria for new debt. This can happen even while your company is increasing rapidly in value. Unfortunately, financing sources tend to be wary of that combination of distorted cash flow and depleted working capital caused by growth.

Is there a solution?

Yes—at least a partial one. In order to soften the cash flow and capital problems, you have to look ahead. Try to prepare for the crunch before it comes and trim costs accordingly.

One way to accomplish this is to use variance reports. A variance report displays variations in performance from previously established performance guidelines. These are usually drawn from cash flow budgets and income statement projections.

Variance reports, prepared regularly (usually monthly or weekly):

Compel attention to budgets without excessive attention to detail. Budgets are often ignored because of the detail involved. The variance report system minimizes detail and maximizes useful information. You are able to detect serious variations. Then, and only then, is it necessary to draw on detailed information.

Help focus your attention on real problems. Most of us use our time inefficiently. One of the best uses of your time is solving problems that affect the business *before* they get out of hand. If the variance report shows a cost slipping out of control or a new efficiency in production, you know where to direct your efforts.

Provide the basis for evaluating performance. Variance reports are highly effective teaching tools. A department that consistently achieves or exceeds the standards implicit in these reports merits attention. What is being done well? A department that consistently misses poses other problems.

Help you and your financial advisors look ahead to avert cash flow and capital problems. One of the most common problems for a growing company is that as sales and output go up, costs slide out of control. This may be due to a number of subtle causes, but most of the time, it's because basic cost information is ignored. Variance reports allow you to set cost guidelines, and follow major costs.

Your application of variance reports will be unique. Be sure to get competent professional help establishing standards and guidelines if you think you need it In most businesses that have never used a variance report system, the cost of professional help and implementation will immediately be offset by the savings.

Acquire Cost Data

The least expensive way to get this information is to rely on your accountant. Doing it yourself is an essay in reinventing the wheel. Most likely, your business will need to be examined operation by operation.

This is less difficult than it may sound. What you need to know is:

1. how long the operation takes and how that time is distributed (work flow analysis helps here);

2. what that time costs—including idle time, pauses, interruptions and so forth;

3. what materials costs are involved;

4. what administrative overhead costs are for the operation.

If you attempt to design a system to get these costs, you'll drown in detail. Pay your accountant to do it, unless, of course, you have a cost accountant on your staff.

Aim to put realistic time and dollar costs on each product or service. As you and your accountant plow through the cost data and discuss operations with your employees (who will usually have good ideas on how to improve work flow), you will begin to spot opportunities for immediate savings. This is an instant bonus—but the real savings will show up later, when budgets based on actual times and costs are implemented.

Suppose you have four different product lines. Do you know which ones are profitable? Which are less profitable? Which are predictable and which are not? Why? Your accountant should be able to provide this level of information—it's important.

Unless you know how much a product or service costs, and why it costs that much, you can't control costs (and benefit from the learning curve as you begin to understand the process more deeply) and you can't price your product or service effectively. More than one company has energetically expanded sales of items they were losing money on, while ignoring profitable ones.

Prepare Monthly Income Statement and Cash Flow Projections

These projections allow you to establish useful budgets.

Why do you need both? To help you achieve the aims of any budget: preservation of liquidity and advantageous use of available capital.

Your income statement projections contain, in condensed form, sales and expense information. Since these ultimately affect your balance sheet (in the long run, profits from operations are the only way to make the business grow), you need income statements to show how long-term debt will be repaid. These projections are also important if you're going to need capital investments, whether the capital is yours or someone else's.

In the shorter term, the income statement helps avert cash flow and liquidity problems by flagging sales lags (or increases) and expense variances. Used monthly, your variance reports:

1. display the information in your projections;

2. let you know whether your projections are being met;

3. help you predict cash flow difficulties before they hit.

A sales problem in March can surface as a cash problem in June. If you are aware of the problem by early April, you have ample time to explain to your banker why you'll need short-term funds.

The cash flow projection, on the other hand, is almost exclusively attuned to short-term needs. These projections become your budget. Your projections will become more accurate with experience and good cost data. Strive to improve them—otherwise they're doomed to be just fun with numbers.

Cash flow projections are the single most important financial control for most

---

Figure 8.1

Variance Report
Month of_____ , 19—

	Projected	Actual	Variance
Net Sales	_____	_____	_____
Cash Receipts	_____	_____	_____
Cash Disbursements	_____	_____	_____
Cash Surplus or Deficit	_____	_____	_____
Cash Balance—Month End	_____	_____	_____
Short-Term Debt Required	_____	_____	_____

COMMENTS/PROPOSED ACTION: _____

_____

_____

Signature _____

Date _____

---

small and growing businesses, but they need to be supported by income statements if the business is to become stable and profitable. We recommend that you use both.

Prepare Variance Reports

The variance report can be taken directly from the income statement and cash flow projections. Any variance can be tracked to its source with a minimum of effort. If you think you need more detail, then the process is the same.

What you exclude may be as important as what you include, since an exhaustive variance report that tracks down individual paper clips is sure to be ignored while a report that does not account for labor costs will be completely useless. Attempt to strike a balance.

What are the important variables you want to keep on top of?

What items can be combined or ignored?

As with most management tools, variance reports become more useful as you use them more. The key is to begin to use them as soon as possible, even if they are only 85% accurate. The pursuit of 100% accuracy probably keeps a few of your competitors from using them at all.

Figure 8.2

Production Variance Report
Month of _____ , 19—

	Projected Orders	Actual Orders	Variance
Product A	_____	_____	_____
Product B	_____	_____	_____
Product C	_____	_____	_____

COMMENTS/PROPOSED ACTION: _____

_____

_____

_____

_____

Signature _____

Date _____

If you were limited to ten pieces of information about operations, what would they be? The number is arbitrary, but the point is that too much information is as bad as too little. Then ask: What standards (expressed in dollars) do I need to keep track of these activities?

Track Key Financial and Operating Ratios

The trends of your ratios can be a profitable study. Your monthly financial statements should allow you to calculate all of the ratios in Figure 8.3. If you then examine them as they change over a period of three months, and discuss them with your banker, you should be able to spot coming liquidity and/or capital problems.

Three key ratios to follow are the current ratio, debt-to-worth, and pre-tax profit/sales. The current ratio measures ability to meet short-term debts. The debt-to-worth ratio measures ability to assume more long-term debt. Pre-tax profit/sales ratio measures ability to retire long-term debt.

Your banker will almost certainly wish to follow these ratios over a period of months—the concerns are similar to yours: can you handle the debt? Are you managing your company efficiently? This would be indicated in part by improving ratios.

Decide what you would like the ratios to be from your forecasts and pro-formas. Then check monthly to see how you are doing—is there a significant deviation? If so, is it good or bad? This is another way to apply deviation analysis to your business' performance.

Fill Out Variance Reports Regularly, at least Monthly

Timely information is a lot more valuable than stale information. That's why variance reports are useful: they demand repeated comparison of actual performance against stated goals while this information is still useful.

Variance reports take minutes to complete . . . and years to apply.

Of course, if the necessary information is not available on a monthly basis, or comes in six weeks after the end of the month, you have a different kind of problem. At the very least, you should have prompt monthly information on budgets, sales, production, and selected variable expenses. If your system doesn't provide these, change your system.

Take Action as Indicated

The sole use of any management tool is to guide action—intelligently.

All a variance report can do is to make you aware of a variance. It won't lead you to the cause, or tell you what action to take.

Figure 8.3

Ratio Analysis Trends Chart

Name	Formula	Month 1	Month 2	Month 3	Comments
Current Ratio	Current Assets/Current Liabilities				
Quick Ratio (Acid Test)	Cash & Mkt. Sec. & Accts. Rec./Current Liabilities				
Debt-to-Worth	Total Debt/Tangible Net Worth				
Cash Earnings Coverage	Net Profit & Depreciation/Current Maturities LTD				
Receivables Turnover	Total Annual Sales/Accounts Receivable				
Days Sales Outstanding	360 Days/Receivables Turnover				
Inventory Turnover	Total Annual Cost of Sales/Inventory				
Days Inventory	360 Days/Inventory Turnover				
Payables Turnover	Total Annual Purchases/Accounts Payable				
Days Payable Outstanding	360 Days/Payables Turnover				
Return on Assets	Pre-Tax Profit/Total Assets				
Return on Investment	Pre-Tax Profit/Tang. Net Worth				
	Pre-Tax Profit/Sales				
	Gross Margin/Sales				
Income Statement Ratios	Annual Sales/Monthly Sales				
	Interest Exp./Sales				

If you have carefully identified the key variables in your business, and have based your projections and budgets on experience and good cost information, the variances will be minimal. Some measures are more sensitive than others. It may be useful to divide costs into those that are controllable, those that might become controllable, and those that cannot be controlled. Your aim is to move as many as possible into the controllable column. Sometimes this can be done simply by keeping a sharp eye on them. Costs that go unnoticed always increase.

There are several ways to get a line on which costs need to be more firmly controlled. One is gross dollar amount. Look into any costs over an established dollar amount. Another is fixed vs. variable cost analysis. Fixed costs don't need to be scrutinized as often as variable costs, which are more closely associated with sales levels. Another method is percentage deviation. Any variances over 5%, for example, are examined; any over 8% require immediate action.

A variance report is a guide to action. Get the report each month, study it, think about what the variances imply, then take action. If, for example, sales are down this month, but unit costs are up, you'll want to find out why. Maybe sales are down because of new competition. Maybe the pricing structure needs adjusting. Perhaps a salesman is goofing off. Maybe sales were increasing by the end of the month and will level out over the quarter.

All a variance report can do is wave a red flag at you. Once you know what the symptom is, you can look for a cause and a cure. The unseen problems are the ones that can destroy a business.

Review System Periodically; Revise as Needed

As with any system, variance reports become rusty after a while. Circumstances change. Cost structures alter, new equipment and competition change the picture. Expenses surge as sales volume increases.

Hence the need to update the system periodically, at least annually. Review plans for the coming year, and make adjustments as necessary.

Summary

Variance reports won't take up much of your time. They don't cost much. They don't require a huge front-end investment. And they pay off. If your budgets don't work as well as you'd like them to, try variance reports. By checking performance against budgets monthly, you make sure that the budgets work over the course of a year. This is especially important for a growing company, since growth depletes both liquidity and bankability due to the erosion of ratios. Variance reports won't prevent these problems, but they'll help you diminish their impact.

Action Plan For:
Financial Controls

☐ Acquire cost data. You can control expenses more easily than revenue.

☐ Prepare monthly income statements and cash flow projections.

☐ Prepare variance reports monthly (or more often).

☐ Compare financial and operating ratios, every month, against the standards you have set.

☐ Take action as indicated. You have to decide how large a variation is acceptable before you act.

☐ Review your system periodically: Revise them as needed, usually once a year.

Chapter Nine:

Deviation Analysis

....

Y our cash flow budget, established and tested over time, helps you to keep a close grip on your actual (as opposed to estimated) performance.

There are two ways to do this.

First, be casual. Eyeball the budgeted figures and compare them with what you think you have done over the period. This has the advantage of simplicity if not accuracy, and is better than doing nothing at all.

Better: Take the time to do a thorough job of looking for significant deviations. The actual time investment is not that great. One evening a month is more than adequate for most small businesses.

We strongly recommend the more formal approach because it works. It makes sure that you use your budget It helps steady your control over your business. That's the first and most important use of your budget.

This formal approach is called "Deviation Analysis."

If you have more than one source of sales, you may benefit from preparing separate budgets for each profit center. This way you can control them better—and find out where your profits are really generated.

Deviation analysis provides the warning signs when your business begins to drift away from the charted course. It also tells you when you are doing well, and can help you latch onto possibilities you might never spot otherwise.

Enter Actual Monthly Figures on
Deviation Analysis Forms (both P&L and Cash Flow)

Deviation Analysis is best performed as soon as current figures are available. Don't wait until the figures become stale. If filling out the forms and spotting the deviations takes more than a few hours, something has gone wrong. (Usually the budget, though not necessarily.)

Deviation Analysis puts your managerial task into sharp focus; here is a problem, there is an opportunity. As the owner or manager it is your job to decide what to do. One measure of how well your business is being run is to compare time spent seeking new profit areas to time spent solving last month's problems. You have to solve the problems first, so the fewer problems, the greater the chance to find new profits.

You'll need a Profit & Loss Projection and a Cash Flow Budget. You must also know what expense and income categories are most appropriate for your business. Those indicated in the forms are (at best) a beginning. Customize the form and fit it to your business.

Assuming that you have performed these necessary steps, the first part of monthly deviation analysis is simple. Enter the Actual figures for the period in Column A.

After entering the sales and expense information on the P&L, and the cash sales and other cash inflows and disbursements on the Cash Flow Budget, anomalies will begin to appear. With experience, you will notice when sales are changing their complexion—when a slight rise in credit sales begins, the P&L sales will be higher than usual, cash sales lower. The difference may not be great, but it will show clearly.

For expenses and disbursements, the same kind of patterns will develop. If expenses rise, but cash disbursements do not, then you know that your payables are increasing. There may be excellent reasons for this—say, laying in a seasonal inventory, or enduring a seasonal shift in your oil bill. But these are matters which you must be aware of, and even such obvious matters can slide by.

Both the cash flow and the P&L have lessons for you . If you heed both, you'll help yourself.

Enter Budgeted Figures
on Both Monthly Forms (Column B)

If you have not made a P&L budget, the best way to do so is to go back to the projected annual P&L—the basis of your cash flow budget.

Most of the items on a projected P&L are based on a combination of:

a. experience;

b. anticipated changes for the next year (preferably documented and carefully reasoned);

c. industrial averages such as NCR, Robert Morris and trade figures.

Since the P&L projection is at the center of your business plan, it is a must do item. Your projected P&L is the numerical expression of the plans you have made for your business. For anyone who wants to achieve profit goals and control the ordinary expenses which bleed profits in almost every business, time spent carefully establishing these projections will be repaid many times over.

Your projected P&L gives annual totals for each item—each product or service line and all expense items.

Divide these line totals by 12. This assumes that each month approximately 1/12th of the annual budget will be spent. Naturally, this is misleading—the cash flow budget makes the adjustments for timing, and of course, no company has such a regular income and expense flow as the P&L budget expresses.

No matter. If there is a major seasonal fluctuation, or a proposed major asset acquisition (or any major change in your business), adjust your P&L budget to suit the change. Do not get bogged down in too much detail. Overplanning is as feckless as not planning at all. Expenses such as legal and accounting, insurance, dues, licenses and fees should be allocated evenly throughout the year.

This is one area where you should use your bookkeeper and accountant. You provide the outlines. They provide the details. Tell them what you need by way of information—and concentrate on running your business. But you have to scrutinize the figures on the forms. They serve as constant reminders of your budget, and can spur you to make sensible economies or intelligent investments. There is no substitute for organized, coherent review of your entire business on a consistent, periodic basis.

Calculate Dollar Amount of Deviation (subtract Column A from Column B for Column C)

You need to know the dollar deviation from the budget amounts. Subtract the Actual from the Budgeted (Column A from Column B) to arrive at the change. Enter in Column C. Decide well in advance which deviations are and are not acceptable. Also make notations of acceptable levels or ranges of deviation for future reference.

Calculate Percent Deviation, Multiply Result by 100

This is purely mechanical—but again it affords a chance to think about each income and expense item, each cash inflow and outflow.

Figure 9.1

Deviation Analysis
Profit & Loss

Month_____

	A: Actual for Month	B: Budget for Month	C: Deviation B-A	D: % Deviation C/B x 100
SALES				
LESS: Cost of Goods				
GROSS PROFIT ON SALES				
OPERATING EXPENSES:				
VARIABLE EXPENSES				
Sales salaries (commissions)				
Advertising				
Miscellaneous variable				
TOTAL VARIABLE EXPENSES				
FIXED EXPENSES				
Utilities				
Salaries				
Payroll taxes & benefits				
Office supplies				
Insurance				
Maintenance & cleaning				
Legal & accounting				
Delivery				
Licenses				
Boxes, paper, etc.				
Telephone				
Miscellaneous				
Depreciation				
Interest				
TOTAL FIXED EXPENSES				
TOTAL OPERATING EXPENSES				
NET PROFIT				
TAX EXPENSES				
NET PROFIT AFTER TAXES				

Figure 9.2

Deviation Analysis
Cash Flow

Month_____	A: Actual for Month	B: Budget for Month	C: Deviation B-A	D: % Deviation C/B x 100
BEGINNING CASH BALANCE				
ADD: Sales Revenue				
Other Revenue				
TOTAL AVAILABLE CASH				
DEDUCT: Estimated Disbursements				
Cost of materials				
Variable labor				
Advertising				
Insurance				
Legal & accounting				
Delivery				
Equipment*				
Loan payments				
Mortgage payment				
Property tax expense				
DEDUCT: Fixed Cash Disbursements				
Utilities				
Salaries				
Payroll taxes & benefits				
Office supplies				
Maintenance & cleaning				
Licenses				
Boxes, paper, etc.				
Telephone				
Miscellaneous				
TOTAL DISBURSEMENTS				
ENDING CASH BALANCE				

CALCULATIONS: A. ADD current month actual to last month's year-to-date analysis.
B. ADD current month budget to last month's year-to-date analysis.
*Equipment expense represents actual expenditures made for purchase of equipment.

Figure 9.3	**Deviation Analysis** **Profit & Loss**			
Year-To-Date_____	A: Actual YTD	B: Budget YTD	C: Deviation B-A	D: % Deviation C/B x 100
SALES LESS: Cost of Goods GROSS PROFIT ON SALES				

OPERATING EXPENSES:
VARIABLE EXPENSES
  Sales salaries (commissions)
  Advertising
  Miscellaneous variable				

TOTAL VARIABLE EXPENSES				

FIXED EXPENSES
  Utilities
  Salaries
  Payroll taxes & benefits
  Office supplies
  Insurance
  Maintenance & cleaning
  Legal & accounting
  Delivery
  Licenses
  Boxes, paper, etc.
  Telephone
  Miscellaneous
  Depreciation
  Interest				

TOTAL FIXED EXPENSES				
TOTAL OPERATING EXPENSES				
NET PROFIT				
TAX EXPENSES				
NET PROFIT AFTER TAXES				

Figure 9.4	**Deviation Analysis**			
		Cash Flow		
Year-To-Date_____	A: Actual YTD	B: Budget YTD	C: Deviation B-A	D: % Deviation C/B x 100
BEGINNING CASH BALANCE				
ADD: Sales Revenue				
Other Revenue				
TOTAL AVAILABLE CASH				
DEDUCT: Estimated Disbursements				
Cost of materials				
Variable labor				
Advertising				
Insurance				
Legal & accounting				
Delivery				
Equipment*				
Loan payments				
Mortgage payment				
Property tax expense				
DEDUCT: Fixed Cash Disbursements				
Utilities				
Salaries				
Payroll taxes & benefits				
Office supplies				
Maintenance & cleaning				
Licenses				
Boxes, paper, etc.				
Telephone				
Miscellaneous				
TOTAL DISBURSEMENTS				
ENDING CASH BALANCE				

CALCULATIONS: A. ADD current month actual to last month's year-to-date analysis.
B. ADD current month budget to last month's year-to-date analysis.
*Equipment expense represents actual expenditures made for purchase of equipment.

Fill in Year-to-Date Forms (both P&L and Cash Flow)

This step is also mechanical—fill in the columns, keeping a running total by adding this month's figures to last month's Year-to-Date figures.

By doing this, you multiply the effectiveness of your monthly deviation analysis. The monthly forms help identify sharp deviations, those caused by sudden shifts or unforeseen events. But the slow, subtle trends are apt to slide by the month-by-month analysis; the **Year-to-Date** forms highlight these trends.

Changes are inevitable, but if the changes are taking place without your knowledge, they can result in unhappy surprises and missed opportunities. If you know about them, then you can take action as required.

Up to this point, the review has been largely mechanical. It's a simple matter to enter numbers on a form, and as indicated above the forms could be filled out by your bookkeeper.

But from here on in, it's your job as owner or manager to *use* the information. *This cannot be delegated.*

Determine Acceptable Deviation Limits

1. Determine what **Total** or **Absolute** dollar deviation is acceptable.

2. Determine what percentage deviation is acceptable.

3. Decide well in advance what deviations are and are not acceptable.

Compare P&L and Cash Flow

This step has four distinct sub-steps. Look for:

1. deviations appearing on both sets of forms;

2. deviations appearing on just P&L or just Cash Flow forms;

3. trends as opposed to spot occurrences;

4. deviations which are under your control, and deviations which are not.

Deviations appearing on **both** sets of forms are clearly red flags. These are (usually) unforeseeable fluctuations, major problem areas, or, if positive, situations you wish to encourage. The principle: Spot the deviation first, then you can find out why it has occurred.

Suppose the deviation is on the P&L but not on the Cash Flow. Several possibilities are common—a bill has been forgotten or paid too soon. An expense was unanticipated, and will show up on a future cash flow. An expense proved unnecessary, and won't appear later. There are any number of possibilities—but if you can track down the cause of the deviation, you can't help but be ahead.

Suppose the deviation shows in the Cash Flow but not on the P&L. Again, there are many possible reasons—bills paid too soon or not at all (or never incurred), unexpected purchases, new personnel costs. But by going over each item, including the Fixed cash disbursements, the cause will soon be spotlighted. Then you can decide what to do before the problem grows too large or an opportunity slides away.

Don't waste time trying to effect changes in events beyond your control.

By looking carefully at the monthly, then the year-to-date forms, you'll spot the trends that may be small each month, yet represent a significant sum over a period of time.

That brings us to the final consideration. Which deviations are controllable? Which are not?

Don't waste time trying to effect changes in events beyond your control. If you don't know what's happening to your business, as reflected in the constant updating of information in the deviation analysis, you can't do more than be pushed to and fro.

Determine Course of Action, Implement and Review

By now you will know where your business is deviating from the planned path, what kind of deviation you have to deal with—and whether you can do anything about it.

Once you have decided to pursue a course of action, prompted by your specific knowledge of what needs to be done and why, implement the new course.

However, you must review the implementation, which may involve reworking your budgets while continuing to perform deviation analysis.

Since deviation analysis is based on **budgets**, changes in your budgets affect the analysis.

Long-range, the goal is to manage your business better. This may mean more profitably; deviation analysis helps cut costs and increases your ability to spot opportunities for new business. Both add to your bottom line.

Summary

Deviation analysis is a technique that takes little time and yields excellent results.

The mechanical part may be done by any person who is thorough—but the most important parts, setting limits to work within and making sure the limits are observed, are your job. You can't delegate this; the responsibility has to be yours.

The goal is to make your job more manageable. As you practice deviation analysis, you will find that you have more time to spend improving your company, and won't have to spend so much time cleaning up yesterday's problems. It works.

Action Plan For:
Deviation Analysis

Each month:

☐ Enter actual monthly figures on deviation analysis forms (both P&L and Cash Flow).

☐ Enter budgeted figures on both monthly forms (Column B).

☐ Calculate dollar amount of deviation (subtract Column A from Column B for Column C).

☐ Calculate percent deviation. Multiply result by 100.

☐ Fill in Year-to-Date Forms (both P&L and Cash Flow).

☐ Look for any items (on each form) where the deviation from standards or budgets is significant enough to come to your attention.

☐ Compare P&L and Cash Flow.

☐ Determine course of action, implement and review.

Chapter Ten:

Interim Financial Statement Analysis

....

You don't have to be a financially trained person to benefit from analyzing your company's interim financial statements. You want to be consistent and look at your monthly statements (income statement and balance sheet) with an eye to changes from one month to the next.

Each month, take ten figures from the most current financial statements available to you.

Calculate ten simple (arithmetic) ratios and follow them from month to month.

So much for the analysis. The next step is to use the trends and ratios as information to help you make decisions.

Unlike your banker, you won't be concentrating on the so-called "safety" ratios such as "Times Interest Earned" or "Cash Flow/Current Maturities of Long Term Debt." While these are extremely important, their function is to assess the ability of a company, based on the experience of the industry that business is in, to handle additional debt load.

And unlike an investor in the stock market you won't be looking for earnings ratios or complicated balance sheet footnotes showing changes in accounting methods that could alter the meaning of the figures. Working with interim statements for operating purposes has a different method.

Hence this topic. It is not a substitute for the more thorough analyses of financial statements that you do once or twice a year. Its sole purpose is to provide a simple, fast method of putting information gained from interim financial statements into a form that can be used to guide short-term operating decisions.

Create Monthly Balance Sheet and Income Statements

You may not be using monthly balance sheets and income statements—many executives prefer to rely solely on cash flow budgets and deviation analysis to manage their businesses in the short term.

While a cash flow budget is a necessity in every business, and deviation analysis is a nifty method of implementing and using that budget, these techniques provide only part of the picture. Your balance sheet, used in conjunction with your income statement, provides information about ability to meet current obligations (liquidity measures), effectiveness of your sales and collection efforts, asset management, and profitability of current operations. These are obviously handy measures— and they take very little time and effort to generate. Your bookkeeper can produce them within a few days of month's end, as soon as the statements are available. If you have a computerized general ledger system, you can generate interim statements almost instantaneously at any time of the month.

The balance sheet, showing how your company's assets and liabilities were distributed as of the last day of the preceding month, is often compared to a snapshot: it freezes the action, shows the results of the operations of the business as of a certain date, and provides a baseline from which to measure changes.

The income statement is a more dynamic indicator of operations. It shows sales, gross margin, and, of course, profits for a specific time frame. The changes in the income statement show up in the balance sheet as reallocation of assets and liabilities: if the company is making a steady profit the balance sheet will show it in increased assets and/or reduced liabilities, and in increasing net worth.

Since the income statement shows expenses and sales as they occur rather than when the bills are paid or the sales turn into cash, it affords a different kind of measure than the cash flow statement. In many ways the income statement is a less sensitive measure when taken alone, but taken in conjunction with income statements from prior time periods and from industry averages, it helps you identify directions of some trends. When used with the comparable balance sheet, an income statement is even more revealing. In expert hands it can show where money came from and where it went as well as non-cash expenses such as amortization or depreciation.

There are additional reasons why you may need frequent financial statements. Your budgets may be based on the income projections rather than the cash flow projections. The discipline of assembling monthly statements makes you pay more attention to fixed expense control, a phenomenon that many business owners ignore to their woe. Sales fluctuations are spotted more quickly, as are aberrations in controllable expenses.

Determine Key Ratios and Trends in Your Business

The spreadsheets in Figures 10.1 and 10.2 provide for the calculation of ten key ratios which any business would find useful, plus room to examine seven key balance sheet items and three key income statement items. These 20 measures were not picked lightly; their importance will be discussed below.

You almost certainly will have other ratios or financial statement items that you want to track. Our advice is to keep the number to a minimum, though—too many "key" measures can be as misleading as none. Suppose, for example, that your business extends a great deal of credit, much of it to questionable accounts. Knowing how many days receivables are outstanding would be helpful—but you would want more detailed information, perhaps broken down in an aging of the receivables, showing the status of accounts receivable of 40 days, 50, 60, 70, 80, 90 and over.

For ordinary monthly operations management, the fewer items to follow the better.

What are the ten items you should follow?

1. Cash and Near Cash

The availability of highly liquid assets is vital to the survival of most companies. You need cash to pay ongoing expenses including payroll, taxes, and other current liabilities.

Changes in these accounts need close attention. You want to minimize idle cash yet maintain liquidity. You may be able to use a cash management system centered on a zero balance checking account or some kind of investment account. Ask your banker.

Excess cash may indicate bills not paid, early payments by your customers, new investment or debt, sale of a fixed asset or any number of possibilities. What is important is that you are prepared. If the cash is low, the same kinds of thinking apply. Ask why. Maybe sales or receivables collection has fallen off. Or a major asset has been purchased with cash—or a bill prepaid, suppliers demanding cash on delivery, or some other problem.

2. Accounts Receivable

While these are close to cash, they can't be used to pay bills unless you collect them, borrow against them, or sell them.

Any change in receivables this month affects next month's operating cash flow—assuming standard 30 day terms—so an increase or decrease has serious implications. Forewarned is forearmed. Track your receivables.

Receivables rising? Maybe sales are up. Or collection efforts are down. Or the market is shifting towards more extensive use of credit, or sales are being made to a different market segment.

Receivables down? This could signal better collections, lowered sales, downturns in the business climate, tightening of credit standards, or higher cash sales.

3. Inventories

These are even further removed from cash. If inventories represent a substantial portion of your company's current assets, this could be a major index of future operating concerns: lowered inventories can mean better use of as-needed or JIT (just in time) inventory management. Lowered inventories could also indicate that a reorder point was missed, a line dropped, or that an unusual order put pressure on the inventory and the delivery of new inventories hasn't yet occurred.

Higher inventories could mean a sales slump, careful stockpiling against anticipated production needs, careless ordering, or wise investment against a price rise or shortage.

Once more, the key is to be aware that something is happening.

4. Current Assets and Total Assets

These are more useful for ratio calculation than for operating purposes, although a sudden change in either of these would indicate a need for further examination. Usually the changes in, for instance, a lower inventory will show up as higher cash or receivables, leaving the totals unchanged.

5. Current Liabilities

As these rise and fall monthly, you have to follow them. If they fall, you may be retiring debt or paying bills too swiftly, may have forgotten to place an order, may have missed posting a bill. Or maybe cash flow has improved, enabling you to catch up and get ahead of liabilities, take trade discounts and lower your costs. The change from normal triggers the question: Why?

Suppose current liabilities are higher this month than last. You may have assumed new debt, ordered additional inventory, be gearing up for higher sales due to the seasonality of your business. Again: awareness of the change triggers your questions.

6. Total Debt

Changes in debt level (other than new debt) are indirectly tied to operations, but since debt is ultimately repaid from operating profit, you need to keep an eye on it.

Your banker will be interested in changes in the amount of debt your company carries. Too much debt is dangerous; too little may indicate overly cautious financial management resulting in lower sales and loss of market share.

7. Net Worth

If your business is making money, this tends to rise. If you're losing money on operations, this falls—and since in many ways net worth is an ongoing report card on overall management you should monitor it closely. Your banker does.

8. Sales

The implications of fluctuations here are obvious. You know that if sales are steadily rising or falling, your cash flow will change predictably. So will the work flow and other operating concerns; inventories will have to be adjusted, personnel hired or laid off and so on.

However, sales for many businesses are seasonal, and if you don't know the pattern for your business, you could be making unwise decisions.

Sales increases or decreases this month will affect next month's balance sheet—and the balance sheet items have a direct bearing on the level and profitability of sales you can afford At least quarterly, you and your accountant or treasurer should carefully examine changes in the balance sheet and in sales and expense. Ask for a funds flow statement and an explanation.

But on a monthly basis, your concerns are simpler. What is happening to sales? Are they rising or falling? What will happen next month (to make sure that your operation is ready to meet that sales level)? Why?

9. Gross Margin

Almost as important as the sales figure, the gross margin shows how well operations are being performed.

Gross margin is figured by subtracting the Cost of Sales from Gross Sales. Since the cost of sales goes up or down with sales (usually though not always with perfect synchrony), the amount of revenue available to meet fixed expenses is governed by this figure. Careless production, for example, will show up as higher cost of sales. Sloppy work flow, careless ordering of raw inventories, and short-term cost problems tend to cluster here.

Rising margins are desirable. Lowered margins aren't—unless there is a good reason for the change, such as increased training costs.

10. Net Profit

The bottom line. If the trend of profits is upwards, good. If not, bad. And in either case, changes call for asking why.

However, constant attention to short-term profit is foolish. While you would normally want constant profitability, the costs, for example, of increasing volume, including new debt service to cover plant and equipment training costs for new or promoted personnel, administrative costs to establish a new branch office—and so on—can erode short-term profitability.

Furthermore, "bottom line management" is a cliché—jargon of the worst kind. Profitability is a goal—but long-term profit is one thing, transient profits at the expense of the future quite another. Unless you have the two clearly distinguished, this is a poor measure.

Corresponding to the figures from the financial statements are the ratios that make relationships in the business more understandable. A ratio is only a shorthand note: *this* is what's going on according to your books. If your books are accurate portrayals of your business, the following are the conclusions to think about. Check how they apply to your business by asking your banker, accountant or financial advisors.

1. Acid Test or Quick Ratio:

Cash & Near Cash/Current Liabilities

Measures ability to meet current debt, a stringent test since it discounts the value of inventories. The rule of thumb is 1:1. Lower indicates illiquidity. Higher may imply unused funds.

2. Current Ratio:

Current Assets/Current Liabilities

Another measure of ability to meet current obligations. Less accurate than the acid test for the very near term, but probably a better measure for six months to a year out, since it contains receivables and inventories as well as cash and near cash. Rule of thumb: 2:1, though this will be affected by seasonality.

3. Receivables Turnover:

Sales/Receivables

Measures effectiveness of credit and collection policies. If your ratio is going down, maybe collection efforts are improving, sales are rising, or receivables are being reduced. If going up, sales credit policies may be changing, collection efforts flagging, or sales may have taken a nosedive.

Caution: This ratio depends on when receivables are measured, and the seasonality of the business. Careful bookkeeping is also an essential ingredient. The same applies to Inventory Turnover: make sure that the measures are comparable from month to month. Use average receivables (inventories) if you can.

4. Days Receivables:

30/Receivables Turnover

Another way of looking at receivables. Particularly useful in explaining graphically what changes in credit and collection operations do to a business.

5. Inventory Turnover:

Cost of Goods Sold/Average Inventory

A measure of how well inventory is managed. Most businesses have a steady inventory turn. Compare your figures from year to year, asking yourself what causes the inevitable fluctuations. Small fluctuations are probably due to the flow of work. If you produce one jumbo jet a year your inventory picture will be very different from that of a dealer in ripe tomatoes.

6. Days Inventory:

30/Inventory Turnover

Another way of monitoring inventory. This is controlled by your inventory ordering patterns (among other considerations) so be careful in how you interpret it.

7. Gross Margin:

Gross Margin/Sales

Permits comparison of margins over months with dissimilar sales. Ideally, this holds pretty steady in good months and bad—but it depends on your business. It can distort fluctuations if sales are erratic.

8. Net Profit:

Net Profit/Sales

An overall batting average: the aim is consistency over the long haul, not just short-term stardom.

9. ROI:

Net Profit/Net Worth

Another profitability ratio, best looked at only occasionally, as it tends to magnify short-term shifts in thinly capitalized companies.

10. ROA:

Net Profit/Total Assets

A better profitability measure than ROI. ROA shows how well are you using your assets.

However, since profits are a volatile short-term measure, this should also be taken with a grain of salt. The long-term trend is what matters. A large investment in new fixed assets to handle growth will seriously alter this ratio.

All ratios must be taken in context. The reason to look at these on a monthly basis is to make sure that you *spot trends as they develop*, not afterwards. If you are doing something exceedingly well, you need to know it And if something is going wrong, better to find out about it sooner than later.

Fill out Spreadsheets

The next step is easy: fill out the spreadsheets. Make copies: you will need several each month to make the best use of the information generated from them.

First, copy last month's COLUMN B into this month's COLUMN A for all three sections (Balance Sheet, Income Statement, Ratio Analysis).

Second, copy this month's figures into COLUMN B.

You will have to calculate this month's ratios—but otherwise all you do is copy 20 numbers and fill in the headings.

Note Changes

This takes a little longer. If you are using a computerized version of the spreadsheet (a simple matter to work out), you can do this automatically.

With a $10 handheld calculator, it takes about ten minutes to make the calculations.

Subtract COLUMN A from COLUMN B. This gives the absolute change to this month from last month—and be sure to indicate the direction of change, positive or negative.

Next, calculate percent change. This will magnify small changes, which can sometimes be helpful.

Finally, fill in the COMMENTS column. If further action is proposed, as in Step Five below, make a note about who is to do what—and by when. This provides an extremely helpful tool for setting priorities; if you are following the right indicators for your business, this effort will more than pay for itself the first time you use it.

Figure 10.1

Income Statement

	A: Last Month	B: This Month	Change (B-A) $	%	Comments
Net Sales					
Cost of Goods Sold					
Gross Margin					
Operating Expense					
Net Profit					

Balance Sheet

Cash					
Near Cash					
Accounts Receivable (Net)					
Inventory					
other					
Total Current Assets					
Fixed Assets					
Total Assets					
Current Liabilities					
Total Liabilities					
Net Worth					

Take Action as Appropriate

One action you should take is to keep these spreadsheets from month to month, as a constant reminder of actions you think should have been taken in the past (or as a record of actions you did take). The cumulative effect of several month's minor improvements in operations can be striking. This is an incremental approach to improving operations, not a quick cure, but it has the advantage of being very controlled.

The spreadsheets will also be helpful when you write your annual business plan and plan strategies for the future, as well as being handy for setting monthly goals.

Ordinarily, based on the experience of people who have followed this kind of management you will have to fight overreacting at first. If you haven't been following these items on a regular basis, it can be a bit unsettling until you get used to discounting unimportant short-term fluctuations. The trick is to separate the unimportant from the important, and that takes a lot of experience.

Figure 10.2

Ratio Analysis Worksheet

	Definition	(A) Last Month	(B) This Month	(B-A) Change	Comments
Acid Test	cash & near cash / current liabilities				
Current Ratio	current assets / current liabilities				
Receivables Turn	sales / receivables				
Days' Receivables	30 / receivables turn				
Inventory Turn	cost of goods sold / average inventory				
Days' Inventory	30 / inventory turn				
ROA	net profit / total assets				
ROI	net profit / net worth				
Gross Margin	gross margin / sales				
Net Profit	net profit / sales				

As with any management technique, this one works only as well as you make it work. It doesn't solve every problem—but it will help you identify operational problems before they swamp you.

Action Plan For:
Interim Financial Statement Analysis

☐ Fill out the spreadsheets for the income statement, balance sheet and key ratios.

☐ Note changes from month to month, both in direction and in amount. Keep your budget standards in mind.

☐ Take action as appropriate.

Chapter Eleven:

Ratio Analysis

....

F inancial ratios help you get a better handle on your operation, see when things are out of kilter, and set down milestones for the future. And once you get the hang of it, it won't take you more than half an hour a month.

Some common concerns are: Do I have enough working capital? Will I be able to make payroll and the next flock of bills? Is my debt too high? Will I have any difficulty meeting my long-term obligations? Am I using my assets wisely? Is my inventory too large, or does it take too long to turn over? How profitable is my business? Financial ratios help you answer these questions and a lot of others.

Those who use ratio analysis say business is a new world for them. Life is a lot easier. They can spend more time working on critical areas instead of guessing which ones need attention. Some people say the beauty of financial ratios is that they provide a report card. If you're doing a good job, you know it. If you're not, you know that, too, and you can do something about it.

One recent convert told us, "Ratios are great because they help you know your business—by making you look at everything."

Some business people don't use ratios because they think they're too much trouble. Or because their accountants don't provide them with the information. Or because they never used them in the past, don't think about them, and don't miss them. Others say they're just too busy buying a truck, getting an order out or taking care of a snafu to worry about the luxury of generating ratios.

The point of this topic is that financial ratios are steaks, not bitter pills. They help you to know what you're doing right as well as what you may be doing wrong. What you do right, you can continue doing. What you do wrong, you can work to correct. As your business grows, you can't shoot in the dark. Learn what **causes** things to work and not work in your business, and you may save yourself hundreds of hours or thousands of dollars.

Ratios aren't magical, so use them with caution. Don't use them mechanically as if, "Well, this must be what's right or wrong with my business because my ratio tells me so."

Ratios are flags. When you compare your latest financial ratio with a standard (past ratios, industry ratios, or future ratios as goals), you can tell whether you are on or off target. If your latest ratio is very close to the standard, it is a yellow flag. It means, "Not bad, keep your eyes and ears open and proceed with caution." If your latest ratio is off target in a positive way, it is a green flag. It means, "Good for you, you're doing something very well. Know why, and go right ahead." If your ratio is out of whack, it is a red flag. It means, "Danger, stop and see if anything is wrong."

Figure 11.1   **Flags**

Red: Off target negative. A possible problem. Danger. Stop and check it out.

Yellow: On target. Keep an eye on it.

Green : Off target positive. A possible strength. Congratulations. Go right ahead.

Key : Know WHY your flags are red, yellow, or green. Identify your problems and strengths.

The process for using financial ratios is easy. Start with your current financial statements. Use them to calculate the financial ratios. These ratios form the basis for important management decisions. Compare the ratios against your standards. Study your red and green flags. Determine their causes. Identify problems and develop solutions. Then, review your new ratios to see how much you've improved.

Thirteen key ratios are used in the financial community, divided into four classes: liquidity, leverage, activity (operations), and profitability.

What are they? Ratios are numbers formed by comparing one component of your business with another—the ratio expresses the relationship between the two. But a ratio in and of itself is of no value; it must be compared to some standard.

Ratio Analysis is to running a business as using a compass is to steering a boat. It helps you to determine your direction so you can reach your destination.

What the Different Ratios Tell You

Liquidity: How liquid am I? Do I have enough working capital? Not enough? Too much?

Leverage: How much debt to equity do I have? Is this good or bad?

Activity: How efficiently do I use my resources?

Profitability: How profitable am I?

Use Current, Accurate Financial Statements

You'll need your income statement (P&L) and your balance sheet. These should be prepared monthly. If you wait too long, a problem could go undetected for many months before you know it. The statements must be timely. And they must be accurate. Inaccurate or corrupt figures are dangerous and misleading.

Financial Statements

Balance Sheet = Snapshot

Freezing action on a certain day, usually end of a period.

Income Statement = Motion Picture

Tells what happened during a period, normally a year, between the starting date and the ending date, say from January 1 to December 31, 19-. **Note:** You need both statements to calculate ratios.

Calculate Liquidity Ratios

Liquidity and leverage ratios are important because they tell you how much "cushion" you've got before you're in trouble.

Liquidity ratios measure how well your current assets cover your current obligations. If you can't cover current obligations, suppliers, creditors, and employees will crowd you until your business begins to shake and crumble.

The problem in projecting cash flow is that it isn't constant throughout the year. It fluctuates. So you've got to have enough of a cushion to cover adverse fluctuations. If your ratios are too low, you could run into a cash flow problem and have trouble meeting payroll and other short run obligations. Pressure from creditors will rise, and this makes for insomnia.

Liquidity Ratios

The Current Ratio and the Quick Ratio (commonly known as the Acid Test) measure your ability to meet your short run obligations.

The **Quick Ratio** or the **Acid Test**. This sensitive ratio gives a quick, simple reading of your short-term liquidity.

$$\frac{\text{Current Assets} - \text{Inventory}}{\text{Current Liabilities}} = \text{The Acid Test}$$

Suppose your Acid Test is .2:1, the industry average is .7:1, and your goal is .7:1. Red flag. You have a liquidity problem. Better increase sales and cut costs.

An old, successful business warrior told us that over the years he could get a sense of how his business was doing by keying into the variations of his Acid Test. It spotlights approaching liquidity problems. As such, it is a great early warning signal for cash flow problems. Again, he was talking about long-term trend analysis, and was tuned into how his financial ratios reflected his business.

The Current Ratio. Inventory is included in the Current Ratio. Since inventory is the least liquid of all assets, and can't be instantaneously changed into cash to pay a bill, this ratio is less precise than the Acid Test.

$$\frac{\text{Current Assets}}{\text{Current Obligations}} = \textbf{Current Ratio}$$

Suppose your Current Ratio is 1.6:1, the industry average 1.8:1, and your goal 2:1. It's not exactly a red flag, but you're not sitting pretty either. Watch things because you're off your goal by 20%. If your inventory makes up most of your current assets, you're in some difficulty because your most liquid assets are in short supply.

Current assets include (in order of decreasing liquidity): cash, short-term securities, accounts receivable, and inventory. A ratio of 1.0 would mean that you would have just enough liquidity to cover your obligations. That figure would be okay if there were no business fluctuations. However, since business does fluctuate, sometimes unpredictably, with the slightest blip you could be behind the eight ball if your Current Ratio were 1.0. So it must be higher; high enough to have a cushion. You can tell how high by looking at industry standards.

Calculate Leverage Ratios

Leverage ratios measure the relationship between debt, assets, and net worth. How much risk do the creditors bear? A second group of leverage ratios is called coverage ratios—they measure the ability of the firm to pay interest expense and other fixed charges annually. They're similar in ways to liquidity ratios. They tell how easily you can pay loan interest. If the cushion is large enough, creditors beam with pleasure because they know they'll get their money back.

We'll look at four leverage ratios: two dealing with debt, assets, and net worth, the second two with coverage.

Leverage Ratios

Total Debt to Total Assets: Divide your total liabilities (short and long-term debt) by your total assets.

$$\frac{\text{Total Debt}}{\text{Total Assets}} = \text{Total Debt to Total Assets}$$

Let's say your Debt/Asset ratio is .8:1 and the industry's is .5:1. Red flag. Debt too high. You will probably have difficulty getting bankers to give you more loans. This might be a good time to go in and talk to your banker.

This is a critical ratio that tells whether the balance of risk is on the side of the creditors or owners. If the ratio is high, there is much more debt than equity, which means that additional bank borrowing might be difficult.

Many owners try to get as much of the operation financed by loans as possible, which shifts the risk to the creditors. If owners finance most of the business themselves, the risk is shouldered by the owners.

The greater the ratio, the greater potential profitability during boom periods. However, in bad times, the chance of loss is greater because the equity cushion might not be enough to keep the business going. Boiled down to the nitty gritty, a high leverage means greater profit to owners during good times (their debtors are receiving monthly payback checks and everyone's happy).

But during bad times, it can be disastrous because additional working capital will have to come from equity infusions or personal loans. If owners can't do that, the business collapses. When leverage is high, things are rosy on the upside. But on the downside (when times are bad), things come to a screeching halt twice as fast. Hence, it is critical that your firm's leverage ratio be well-balanced.

Debt to Net Worth: The Debt to Net Worth ratio is a more direct measure of leverage.

$$\frac{\text{Total Debt}}{\text{Total Net Worth}} = \text{Debt/Worth}$$

If your Debt/Worth ratio is 3.9: 1, the industry's is 3.5:1, your last was 5.2:1, and your goal is 4:1—green flag. You deserve a pat on the back. Great improvement. Your banker will be pleased. Know what you did so you can keep it up.

The same reasoning that applies to the Total Debt to Total Assets ratio applies here.

Times-Interest-Earned: You can tell how easily you can cover your interest payments with this ratio. You can see how you're doing by comparing it with your standards.

$$\frac{\text{Profits before taxes + interest}}{\text{Interest}} = \text{Times-Interest-Earned}$$

Your Times-Interest-Earned ratio is 12:1, your last was 4:1, the industry's is 15:1, your goal is 12:1. Green flag. Not quite the industry average, but another pat on the back. Your earnings are up. Know why and how you did it so you can keep up the good work.

Again, because business is volatile, you must have a large enough cushion to ensure that you can pay your interest. Many loan agreements have a long list of covenants attached. If a covenant is breached, the note or loan holder could bring legal action. Also, if the ratio is too low, you could face difficulty borrowing additional money for an expansion or working capital. So, it's important that you've got a good handle on this ratio.

Fixed Charge Coverage: This ratio is similar to the Times-Interest-Earned ratio, but it also includes your lease payments. These days, leasing is an important part of business, and many of us have long-term leases. The monthly lease payment is like an interest payment—it's quasi-debt. If you don't make this payment, it's just as if you don't make your interest payments. Creditors get uneasy. Consequently, you must know how well you're covering all of your fixed costs.

$$\frac{\text{Profit before taxes + Interest charge + Lease obligation}}{\text{Interest Charge+ Lease Obligation}} = \frac{\text{Fixed Charge}}{\text{Coverage}}$$

How about if your Fixed Interest Coverage is 6.2:1, your last was 2. 1:1, the industry's is 6.5:1, and your goal is 5.8:1? You're right on target. Bull's-eye. No red or green flags.

List Standards for Comparison

By comparing your newly calculated ratios with your last set, with other firms like yourself in the industry, and with ratios you've established as goals, you can get a handle on how you're doing.

Where do you get them? Pick internal ratios off your financial sheets. Calculate your projected ratio goals once a year, based on what's happening in your operation and the economy, and how you feel about what's coming up. There are many sources for industry ratios including Dun and Bradstreet, Robert Morris Associates and trade associations.

What you want are ratios for your industry, in the size and location you're in, monthly if possible, as inexpensively as possible. Industry studies and trends are also useful.

Pick the ratios from the trade sources and list them on your comparison sheet. (See the Ratio Analysis Worksheet, Figure 11.5.) List the ratios from your last set of financial statements (last review). Plug in your projected goals. This provides everything you need to make your analysis.

Compare Liquidity and Leverage Ratios with Standards

Put on your thinking cap. Look at your three standards. Compare your new ratios with them. Note on the form the ratios that are way off target either negatively (red flag) or positively (green flag).

Determine Causes of Liquidity and/or Leverage Problems

This is the second most important part of the analysis. After reviewing your flags, study the red flags. Check for problems and analyze them as closely as you can. Remember, a problem well identified is almost solved.

Figure 11.2

How to Compare Your Ratios with Your Standards

1. Shoot for the **standard.**

2. If you're off, notice the **trend.** Is it up or down? Is this good or bad?

3. Notice the **absolute deviation.** Is it more than 20%, 30%, or 40% off target? (This percentage depends on the ratio you're talking about.) Develop your ability to judge how much a deviation is off, and when you should take action.

4. Compare ratios of **similar situations.** You wouldn't compare the time of an adult man with the time of a young boy for running the mile. Make sure that the firms you are comparing with are the same size, product line and, if possible, area.

5. Watch out for **seasonal differences.**

Study your green flags. Why are your ratios so good? What is it you're doing well? Try to identify it as well as you can. Knowing what you're doing well is as important as knowing what you're doing poorly. You now have powerful information that can help you become more successful.

Develop a Plan and Act on It

This planning includes correcting problems as well as maintaining your strengths. This is the most important step of the analysis. Take action! Don't wait. Time works against you when you have a problem. And if you don't fortify your strengths, they may wither in the future. Develop a plan to correct your problems. Include in your plan a strategy for maintaining your strengths.

Review and Note Changes over Time

Transforming knowledge into action is a major hurdle. Act and check the results of your action by seeing how your ratios have changed at your next review session.

We've all heard the joke that bankers only loan you money when you don't need it. That's overstated, but there's a lot of truth in it Why? Most applications are

Figure 11.3	**How Bankers View Liquidity**	**How Bankers View Leverage**
Low	If chronic, this is often evidence of mismanagement. If your firm were properly managed, you'd have planned for working capital. Often associated with last minute or Friday night financing.	This is a very conservative position. With this kind of leverage, bankers are apt to view your credit demands favorably.
Average	Prima facie evidence of good management. You are using your current assets profitably. When you're customarily in the middle, your banker feels comfortable. No one's going to get concerned.	If your leverage compares favorably with other businesses of your kind and size, bankers are likely to provide some credit because they feel you aren't being pinched by too high a debt load, and you are showing ability to use your resources.
High	Some bankers love it. It's your most conservative position. However, some feel that you're not using your assets hard enough, and are holding too many liquid assets.	If you carry more debt than average, bankers are normally unwilling to loan more unless you can show them extremely good reasons. You may be put on a short-term payout as soon as possible. Any excess liquidity will be called on to retire debt.

for working capital or more long-term debt when the business is illiquid or already heavily leveraged. The ratios are against them; the bank turns them down. Business owners leave the bank grumbling about how bankers only loan them money when they don't need it.

But there's a difference between needing new debt when it appears that you can pay it back, and needing new debt and not easily being able to pay it back.

So get your ratios worked out, know what they mean, and if they're looking bad, plan a trip to see your banker. Keeping in close touch with your banker in bad times as well as good is just good business.

Now turn to the activity and profitability ratios. Activity ratios, sometimes called productivity or operating ratios, answer the question: How efficiently do I use my resources (inventory, accounts receivable, tangible fixed assets, and total assets)? Profitability ratios are your overall report card. They answer the questions: How profitable is my business? How effectively do I manage it?

Calculate Activity Ratios

Activity ratios tell you how effectively you're using the resources at your command. The four resources commonly measured are inventory, accounts receiv-

Figure 11.4

Ratio Combinations		Probable Credit Implications
Liquidity	Leverage	
Low	*Low*	Can usually borrow to satisfy short-term working capital needs, put on a long-term payout basis.
Low	*Average*	May find it difficult to get a short-term loan, to relieve illiquidity.
Low	*High*	Worst case. Forget it. Bankers see such companies as overborrowed, running out of money, and mismanaged. Borrowing would be extremely unlikely.
Average	*Low*	Highly desirable. Banks see you as able to handle additional debt, especially long-term.
Average	*Average*	Your most profitable position, as both resources and credit are being handled well. Proceed with caution, but a good bet. Some credit capacity and, in a crunch, your banker would usually bail you out.
Average	*High*	May get some short-term financing. No long-term, as debt load is too great.
High	*Low*	The best bet from the bank's position but, operationally, this may be too conservative. Will probably be able to get both short and long-term financing.
High	*Average*	A good position. Bankers will help you. Use your cash to reduce your long-term debt, and become even more appealing to credit grantors.
High	*High*	Not a good position. Chances are poor of getting a loan. Use some of your idle cash to reduce your leverage.

Figure 11.5

Ratio Analysis Worksheet

	Future: Projected Goals	External: Industry Averages	Internal: Your Last Ratios	Your New Ratios	Red and Green Flags	Action Taken by/date
Acid Test						
Current						
Debt/Assets						
Debt/Worth						
Times-Interest-Earned						
Fixed Charge Coverage						

able, tangible fixed assets, and total fixed assets. Activity ratios are an essential step toward improving your operating efficiency. The four activity ratios, which are also balancing ratios, are: Inventory Turnover Ratio, Receivables to Sales Ratios, Fixed Asset Turnover Ratio, and Total Assets Turnover Ratio.

Inventory Turnover

Your Inventory Turnover Ratio is a delicate one—it helps you achieve the right balance between overstocking and understocking, which is a fine line, to be sure. If you're overstocked, you're paying interest on working capital as well as paying for products. Don't pay double duty. If you're under-stocked, you could have stockouts, which could give your business a bad image.

Your Inventory Turnover Ratio helps you to walk the tightrope between oversupply and undersupply, while suppliers, customers, and creditors tug you in all directions.

$$\frac{\text{Sales}}{\text{Inventory}} = \frac{\text{Inventory}}{\text{Turnover}}$$

Figure 11.6
Implications of Inventory Turnover Ratio

Too Low:
- Inventory too large
- Poor buying practices
- Under-utilization of working capital
- Extra carrying costs chewing into profits
- Possible theft
- Possible spoiled or outmoded stock

Too High:
- Inventory too small
- Poor buying practices
- Possible stockouts
- Possible skimming of company
- Lack of liquidity/insufficient profitability

Possible Ways to Improve Your Turnover Ratio

To Raise:
- Sell off the spoiled or old inventory
- Examine the size of your order; improve your purchasing techniques
- Improve your marketing

To Lower:
- Order in more economic lots
- Sell off some fixed assets to get cash for inventory
- Cut costs
- Raise prices

When you compare your ratio with your standards, note the deviations. Any large deviation (high or low) in a balancing ratio, such as your Inventory Turnover, is a red flag. You can't go too far in either direction and maintain your balance.

Too low a turnover ratio means your inventory is too large: It's not turning over fast enough. Not only is your inventory costing you extra, but it could indicate theft or old or spoiled stock. It alerts you to poor buying practices, and to buying in uneconomical quantities.

Some owners or managers buy inventory by the truckload (say 2,000 oil filters) because they're getting a discount, without taking into account the carrying cost.

Too high a turnover ratio means your inventory is too small; it raises the specter of a host of possible problems that may not be immediately apparent: poor buying practices, illiquidity, insufficient profits, or stockouts.

Two things you should keep in mind when comparing sales with inventory are price vs. cost and seasonality. Sales are valued by selling price, inventory by cost. Use the cost of goods sold in place of sales to give a purer figure, but check to see how your external standard of comparison has been calculated. If it used price for sales, use price; if cost, use your cost of goods sold. Remember, too, that inventory is seasonal. When comparing your recent ratio with the industry standard, remember that the industry may not reflect seasonal differences. To make your ratio purer, you might have to take an average of your inventory over some set period. Use your judgment here.

Receivables to Sales and Average Collection Period

Your credit policy is one of your important marketing decisions. If your credit is too tight, you lose sales; if too liberal, your carrying costs are high.

You must collect receivables within a reasonable time for them to remain a liquid asset Some may be far from current.

The Receivables to Sales Ratio measures the amount of accounts receivable in relation to sales.

$$\frac{\text{Receivables}}{\text{Net Sales}} = \text{Receivables to Sales}$$

$$\text{Receivables to Sales x 365} = \begin{array}{c}\textbf{Average}\\ \textbf{Collection}\\ \textbf{Period}\end{array}$$

Figure 11.7

Another Balancing Act—Your Credit Policy

No Credit at All	Where You Want to Be	All the Credit in the World
No receivables		Very high sales
No carrying costs		Lots of customers
No cost collection		
		But—
But—		High carrying costs
Lowered sales		High collection costs
		Skyrocketing bad debt expense

Key point: You want a policy that balances potential sales and costs.

When measured against the standards, this ratio tells whether your receivables are high, on target, or low. If high, it might mean that your credit policy is too liberal, or your collection method lax, or possibly both. If low, perhaps your credit policy is too stringent, or your collection procedure too harsh, or both.

The Average Collection Period is calculated by multiplying your Receivables to Sales Ratio by 365, the number of days in a year. This gives your average collection period.

For example, let's suppose sales are $350,000 and receivables are $54,000. Let's calculate the ratios and look at them.

$$\frac{\$\,54,000}{\$350,000} = .15 = \text{Receivables to Sales}$$

0.15 x 365 = 55 days = Average Collection Period

If you find that your collection period is 55 days, the industry's is 36, and your goal was 38, you know you have to take corrective measures. Your credit policy is too liberal, your collection procedure too lax, or both. It's time to look it over.

Industry averages for Receivables to Sales and Average Collection Period ratios indicate the balance that's been found in similar businesses.

Again—it's a high-wire balancing act. Too high or too low a ratio is no good.

Figure 11.8

Aging Schedule

This schedule breaks down receivables according to how long they've been outstanding. For example:

Age of Accounts (Days)	Total Value of Receivables (Percent)
0-20	6
21-30	8
31-45	16
46-60	20
61-90	20
Over 90	20
	Total: 100

The 55-day collection period looks bad in comparison with the industry average. The aging schedule shows the business having serious collection problems with some accounts. If the terms are net 30, 86 percent are overdue, half for over two months. Only a few pay promptly; many are very old. The aging schedule shows that the average account has been outstanding for 55 days; a full 20 percent are over three months old!

Remember, an average doesn't tell you the range, and the oldest receivables are the ones to worry about.

Fixed Asset Turnover Ratio

This important ratio measures the utilization of plant and equipment. It tells how well your firm is using fixed assets relative to other firms in the industry. If the ratio is low, think twice before making new capital investments.

$$\frac{\text{Sales}}{\text{Net Fixed Assets}} = \text{Fixed Asset Turnover Ratio}$$

Suppose your ratio is 2.3, your last was 2.5, the industry's is 5.0, and your goal is 5.2. Red flag. You aren't using your plant and equipment to their full capacity. You might consider selling off some underutilized plant and equipment, or trying to increase sales, or both.

Total Assets Turnover Ratio

This activity ratio measures the turnover of all of your firm's assets. It is calculated by dividing sales by total assets. Total assets equal plant and equipment plus current assets.

This ratio measures whether your firm is generating enough business for its asset investment.

Figure 11.9

Possible Reasons Asset Turnover Ratios Are Off Balance

Too Low:

- Too heavy an investment in fixed assets (ties up capital, pinches growth)
- Extravagance
- Unused capacity
- Using assets as hedge against inflation

Too High:

- Not modernizing, not keeping up-to-date
- Working assets near capacity

Possible Solutions:

- Sell some fixed assets for cash to improve liquidity and leverage, turn to sale and leaseback
- Consider expansion or modernization

$$\frac{\text{Sales}}{\text{Total Assets}} = \text{Total Assets Turnover Ratio}$$

Suppose your ratio is 1.5, your last one was 1.4, the industry average is 2.1, and your goal is 2.0. Red flag. You're well below the external standards and goals. Your company is not generating a sufficient volume for the asset size. Sales should be increased, or some assets disposed of, or both.

An asset turnover ratio that's too low is not always bad. It could indicate a wise investment during inflationary periods—because your assets rise in value with inflation, while your debts decrease in value.

However, it could indicate extravagant spending. You can have the biggest best, and most expensive in office, plant, and equipment, if you have the sales to carry them.

Calculate Profitability Ratios

Profitability Ratios are easy to calculate using your financial statements, and almost impossible to ignore. They answer the bottom line question: How are we doing? Take a hard look at them. They tell you how much money you made on your investment—whether the sky is clear and blue or whether it's falling. They are your overall report card.

There are three ways of measuring profitability: profit margin against sales, against total assets, and against net worth. The three ratios are: **Profit Margin on Sales Ratio, Return on Total Assets Ratio (or ROI)**, and **Return on Net Worth Ratio.**

Profitability is the net result of a large number of business decisions, so these ratios tell how well you manage your business.

Profit Margin on Sales Ratio

The profit margin on sales, calculated by dividing net income after taxes by sales, gives the profit per dollar of sales.

If the ratio is low, it means your prices are too low, costs are relatively high, or both.

This ratio is informative, but it can be misleading. If you have more than one product, you are extremely well-advised to get the help of your accountant, banker, or consultant to help you develop a system for determining product line profitability. Knowing overhead, depreciation, sales costs, and so on, by product line is critical. Without this knowledge, you could have several products that are cutting into your profits and not know about it.

$$\frac{\text{Net Profit after Taxes}}{\text{Sales}} = \text{Profit Margin on Sales Ratio}$$

Suppose your ratio is .04, your last (internal) was .035, the industry average (external) is .05, and your goal (future) is .05. Red flag. You're off by 20 percent. You probably should explore raising your prices, cutting costs, or both.

Return on Total Assets Ratio

This popular ratio, better known as your Return on Investment (ROI), measures the return on the total investment in your business. It includes debt plus equity investment. This ratio can fluctuate widely if you have a narrow asset base, such as in wholesaling. Therefore, you must take into account the kind of business you are in.

$$\frac{\text{Net Profit after Taxes}}{\text{Total Assets}} = \text{ROI}$$

Suppose your last ratio was .06, or six percent, the one before that was five percent, the industry average is ten percent and your goal is nine point five percent. Definite red flag. Your firm is off from the industry average by 40 percent. Try to increase your profit margin and turn over your total assets more quickly.

Return on Net Worth Ratio

This last important ratio measures the rate of return on the owner's investment. It is a more direct measure of profitability because the asset base isn't taken into account. Look at profitability over a longer time frame, perhaps on a yearly basis, to smooth out short-term fluctuations. This ratio doesn't include return on debt, just equity.

$$\frac{\text{Net Profit after Taxes}}{\text{Net Worth}} = \textbf{Return on Net Worth Ratio}$$

If your last Return on Net Worth Ratio was 14 percent, the one before that 13.5 percent, the industry's 15 percent, and your goal 14 percent, bull's-eye—you're right on target.

Use Past Ratios, Industry Ratios, Goals as Standards

Figure 11.10

Three Standards Used in Ratio Comparison

Internal
Last period's ratios

External
Ratios of similar businesses
within the industry

Goals
Projected ratios

Using your financing sheets (P&L and balance sheet), calculate your activity and profitability ratios, and list them on the comparison form. (See Ratio Analysis Worksheet.) Using the trade journals common to your business and standard financial data sources, such as Dun & Bradstreet and Robert Morris Associates, pick off industry averages for businesses of your type and size, and list them on the form. Finally, plug in your projected ratios (goals). These are your standards for comparison and provide you with everything you will need to make your analysis.

Compare Ratios with Standards

Look at your new ratios in comparison to the three standards. Think about any deviations—are there problems? Opportunities?

Studying your deviations is the second most important part of the analysis.

Check them over carefully. Think about them. See if you have either problems or opportunities. If problems, analyze them as thoroughly as possible with your staff. Ferret out the causes. Remember, a problem well-identified is almost solved. Are there any favorable deviations that indicate opportunities? Knowing what you're doing well is as important as knowing what you're doing poorly.

Having determined these causes, you are now armed with powerful ammunition that can help you become more successful.

Develop a Plan of Action

Transforming knowledge into action is the toughest and most important step of the analysis. Take action! If you don't correct your problems, the consequences will be serious. Likewise, if you don't take advantage of opportunities, they will wither on the vine. If you don't move from the stage of knowing to the stage of doing, you will get nowhere.

Develop a well-designed action plan to solve your problems and fortify your strengths.

Review and Note Changes over Time

Monitor your actions by checking the ratios at your next review period. Are you moving in the right direction? Is your plan paying off? Do you need to change it? By constantly monitoring your ratios as they change over time (trend analysis), you can tell if your business decisions are appropriate.

Summary

Ratio analysis helps you to make a wide range of decisions, both short-range ones, such as whether to raise a price or borrow more working capital, and long-range ones, such as whether to expand. You can learn a great deal about your liquidity, ability to obtain more debt capital inventory, credit policy and collection procedures, plant utilization, and profitability. Armed with this information, you'll be able to speak knowledgeably with creditors and investors alike, in bad times as well as good.

Most business owners, even those with math anxiety, are surprised at how easy ratios are to use, how much more they understand about their business and how much better they are able to manage their business.

Try them. You'll be happy you did.

Figure 11.11

Ratio Analysis Worksheet	Future: Projected Goals	External: Industry Averages	Internal: Your Last Ratios	Your New Ratios	Red and Green Flags	Action Taken by/date
Ratio Analysis Worksheet						
Inventory Turnover						
Receivables to Sales						
Average Collection Period						
Fixed Asset Turnover						
Total Asset Turnover						
Profit Margin on Sales						
Net Profit After Taxes (ROI)						
Return on Net Worth						

Action Plan For:
Ratio Analysis

☐ Calculate liquidity, leverage, activity and profitability ratios. Enter them on their respective worksheets so you can measure them against standards (industry or your own).

☐ Determine causes of problems or opportunities that are spotlighted by your ratio analysis. Look for trends as well as absolute differences.

☐ Develop a plan and take action. Assign responsibility; measure results.

☐ Review and note changes over time.

Chapter Twelve:

Credit and Collections

....

Credit and collection policies are difficult to establish since they are tied so closely to cash flow and sales problems. Easier credit terms tend to increase sales, though often at the cost of lower profits if the sales don't turn to cash on time. Tighter credit requirements, on the other hand, are apt to result in fewer sales—and often at the cost of additional profits from those fringe accounts which turn out to be good (although slow) payers.

Set Credit Objectives

Credit policies need to be directed towards some goal. Otherwise selecting the most appropriate type of credit to offer becomes a game of chance, with the concomitant risks of improper credit, needless credit, and avoidable bad debt/cash flow losses.

Why extend credit at all? Look to your business goals. Credit objectives should be derived from your wider business objectives. For example, if you are attempting to penetrate new markets, your credit policy would reflect the importance of acquiring new customers no matter how marginal their credit rating might be. If your marketing decision is to limit the number of customers due to a limited number of account representatives or insufficient production capacity, you would probably set more stringent credit requirements. By limiting credit to only the best risks, you would maximize profits.

You cannot establish the best credit policies for your business until you are clear on what objectives these credit policies are intended to achieve. You cannot set rational credit objectives unless you know where your business is headed.

There are factors affecting credit objectives beyond marketing decisions, too. If your business does not have to extend credit at all—an unusual situation these days—your credit objectives might be to extend no credit at all except under the most compelling circumstances, such as a major customer requesting special accommodation.

The ability of credit departments to make large numbers of credit judgements is also a factor. This has obvious implications for credit policies. You might wish to establish a limit to the number of customers to whom credit should be extended. In the next section we raise the basic question of how much credit you can afford to extend. If you have severe cash flow problems, you may find that you cannot afford to extend credit to anyone.

Ask yourself the following questions:

1. Why should we extend credit?
2. What do we hope to achieve by extending credit (stated in terms of dollars of additional sales, dollars of additional profit, number of customers)?
3. What has our credit policy achieved in the past? This is particularly difficult to answer if records make it difficult to distinguish credit sales from cash sales.
4. What would we ideally achieve by changing our credit policies?
5. What changes in credit policies would lead to these desired goals?

If the methods you are currently pursuing have been paying off, then change them hesitantly, if at all. A system which has worked in the past, that has no glaring faults, is certainly a safer route to follow than any new set of procedures. Bear in mind that any change in credit policy is going to result in difficulties in the sales and credit departments. People develop habits that are hard to change. However, if you ask yourself the set of questions raised above and find that there is good reason to question the effectiveness s of your current credit policies, then seek a set of procedures that will achieve your credit objectives.

The more precise you can make your objectives, the better. If your objective is increased dollar sales, how many dollars? When? How many customers does that represent? Make these numbers as specific as possible and ask yourself if these numbers are attainable in the time allotted.

Determine the credit capacity of your business.

When you extend credit, you are in essence making an unsecured loan to your customers. The basic question is: Can I afford to extend this credit?

To get a rough fix on the amount of credit you extend to your customers, look at your accounts receivable and compare the total with the amount of short term bank debt you carry. If you extend more credit than your business can afford, your short term bank debt will be high relative to the current level of receivables. Look to industry or trade averages to compare performance with your competitors. Ask your banker and accountant. Borrowing from a bank at current interest rates to support slow-paying customers is a sure route to disaster, unless (a) your margins—including reserves for bad debt—are high and (b) you know the costs and can accept them.

Short term debt may be high for other reasons—inventory, bridge financing, or other legitimate short term needs. If, however, you constantly have to borrow against receivables, you would be well advised to sit down with your banker and review your credit policies.

The amount of credit you can afford to extend is directly related to your cash flow. Before you extend credit, ask: What will the impact of delayed receipt of funds be on our ability to pay our own bills? If your cash flow is strong enough to permit extending more credit, then perhaps you should consider relaxing credit restrictions, which creates more accounts receivable. If it is a constant struggle to meet fixed payments, then any way you can accelerate cash flow—which includes turning accounts receivable into cash faster—should be vigorously pursued. Tighter credit restrictions will ordinarily accelerate cash flow even though it will reduce total dollar volume.

Figure 12.1

Beware of the Hidden Costs of Extending Credit

Credit is expensive—to you as a creditor, and to the person or business you are extending credit to. Some of the costs are obvious: interest charges to carry accounts receivable, discounts (whether taken or not), and the cost of maintaining a credit and collection department.

Some costs are more subtle. A customer who is past due will often go elsewhere—and pay cash. The strain of worrying about your own cash flow, aggravated by slow paying customers, can be a major problem. Opportunity costs (in missed sales, missed opportunities and chances) can occur due to preoccupation with avoidable problems.

To calculate the direct cost of past due accounts, add up all of those accounts receivable over term. They represent money tied up in funding your customers. It amounts to an interest free loan—unless you charge and collect for the privilege. The 2% finance charge on past due accounts offsets your cost of working capital and places the cost where it belongs. If you do not follow this standard practice you incur unnecessary costs.

Establish and Follow Credit Checking Procedures

The best time to improve collection procedures is before any credit is granted. What do you need to know? In order to extend credit you must know your customers. Some of the principal pieces of knowledge can best be ascertained through your bank. If you tell your bank what credit information you need and why you need it, they will ordinarily provide the information. A standard credit information form is

Figure 12.2

Establishing Credit Limits

There is no mechanical method of allocating credit that we know of. However, a simple policy which works well is to allocate customers to one of the four categories of credit risk (prime, good, average, other) based on past paying behavior, then set a dollar limit for credit less than prime or good customers. Hold to that dollar level unless there is a particularly pressing reason to change it. By selling to average and other credit risks selectively you can increase profits—but you should limit your exposure. This is an area where your banker's experience will help you. The important considerations include: size of order, potential for future orders, kind of product (seasonal, competitive and so on), and status pf present account.

How can you check the credit rating of your customers?

1. Ask your banker to help.
2. Ask your customers to fill out a standard application form.
3. Use the telephone. Vendors are often reluctant to write down negative credit information and may be more forthcoming on the phone once you identify yourself and explain why you need the information.

available from your bank. Adapt it to suit your needs.

Your purpose in performing a credit check on all your customers, not just on your new ones, is to know how much credit those customers can realistically afford to use.

Figure 12.3 is a standard business credit checklist. It does you little good to have the references if you don't check into them. Credit checks are normal business procedure and most business people will be glad to help.

Credit managers divide customers and prospects into four groups: prime customers who provide full operating profits by paying within terms or take discounts; good (70—80% of operating profit); average (50% of operating profit); and other (who expose you to significant delinquency rates and bad debt losses). Naturally you want to sell to as many prime and good customers as possible. Check credit in advance; you can identify these desirable customers. Businesses, like people, tend to follow behavior patterns. Some of the information to get before extending credit is: net worth of the customer, number of employees, name of bank, length of time in business, three or more vendors and the names of principals (see Figure 12.3). For any customer, old or new, you should ask for a credit application. Honest prospective customers will understand the need for credit investigations and will not object.

A surprisingly large number of credit decisions are made irrationally. All of us have hunches and intuitions—but credit experts know that people and businesses who have been poor credit risks in the past will continue to be poor credit risks in the future. You can always ask a prospect to explain a negative credit. You may wish to extend credit in spite of a recent bankruptcy or in the teeth of all rational advice, but at least you will be doing so knowingly and will not be extending credit on whim. If you find that your judgement of credit worthiness is good, follow it. If you find it is not, or you have questions about how good your judgment is, then follow the book.

Manage Accounts Receivable by Carefully Allocating Credit

Now you have allocated each account, present or prospective, to one of the four categories of credit risk. The actual mix of the credit you extend—that is, how many dollars you can afford to extend to each category—can be determined by a combination of calculation and experience. Any standard textbook on financial management will help you determine what kind of profit you can expect from selling on credit to each of these various categories.

Many businesses find it extremely profitable to sell to poor credit risks. Fore those in the "other" category, significant bad debt losses can be anticipated and slow payment is the norm. Such customers frequently cannot get credit and thus are willing to pay a higher price. If the premium they pay for your goods or services outweighs the risk—if you can make money on this group even after absorbing losses for bad debts and increased collection expenses—then it makes good business sense to extend credit to this market. A company that sells to lower categories of credit risks must be structured to handle the problems such a market entails. If your customers tend to be slow paying, then your business should reflect that and so should your credit and collection procedures.

The basic information you need to manage your accounts receivable is gained by aging your receivables,

Figure 12.3

Credit Check List

Customer name: _____

Date: _____

1. D&B rating : _____

2. Trade references* : _____
Talked to: _____
A. Account open since: _____
B. Last sale: _____
C. Terms: _____
D. High credit: _____
E. Amount owing: _____
F. Amount past due: _____
G. Pays within: _____
Comments: _____
_____
_____

Trade References*: _____
Talked to: _____
A. Account open since: _____
B. Last sale: _____
C. Terms: _____
D. High credit: _____
E. Amount owing: _____
F. Amount past due: _____
G. Pays within: _____
Comments: _____
_____

3. Bank Reference: _____
Branch: _____
Officer's name: _____
A. Checking account since: _____
B. Average high: _____
C. Is it a satisfactory account?: _____
D. High credit: _____
E. Payment history: _____
Comments: _____
_____

* We recommend that you check at least two.

which means listing your accounts receivable by due dates: Current, 30 days, 60 days, and over 60 days (for example). If you sell on 30 day terms but your customers pay on 60 day terms and nothing you do can get them to pay faster, you should consider re-evaluating your credit procedures. If you extend 30 day terms and your customers pay within 40 days, you are doing a good job.

To determine the Average Collection Period for your credit sales, divide the dollar total of your annual credit sales by 365. This gives a daily credit sale figure. Divide your total accounts receivable (from your latest monthly financial statement) by the daily credit sales figure; this yields your collection period expressed in days.

Annual credit sales ÷ 365
= Daily credit sales.

Accounts receivable ÷
Daily credit sales
= Collection period in days

The collection period should be no more than 1/3 greater than your net selling terms.

Managing accounts receivable depends on accurate and timely information. Once you know what accounts are outstanding and how much they owe—and whether or not they are current—you should also know, for your own peace of mind, the customary payment practices of those customers, particularly those who owe you large amounts of money. You must closely monitor any potentially dangerous account but unless you are familiar with these accounts you increase risk of bad debt losses. Visit your customers (if possible). Keep an eye on UCC filings. Make sure you have current and accurate financial information on them. Keep track of any sudden, unexpected changes: in purchasing patterns, bank of deposit, personnel,

---

Figure 12.4

Accounts Receivable as Days' Sales

Expressing accounts receivables as days' sales should be included as an analytic technique for comparing company performance against industry standards. This will help you decide when your business might begin to have a credit and collection problem.

As an example, in the medical industry 60 to 62 days collection period is the norm. A medical laboratory which has averaged 59.5 days—a superior performance— might decide to institute changed procedures if their average rises to 61 days, even though that is standard for the industry. Another laboratory might be thrilled to hit 61 days. If their previous performance had been 68 days, the improvement in collection performance would be significant.

It is very important that both the average and the trend for the business be considered. If the collection period is becoming longer. and no other reason can be cited (such as a local economic slump), then the increase is a clear warning to management that collection and credit procedures need review.

Expressing averages in days' sales offers another, lesser benefit: They are easily visualized. This can make a difference—especially if the changes are slight in terms of percentages but amount to a day or more of sales. Once your people can visualize what slackening standards can do, they will make the necessary adjustments in their behavior.

---

or suppliers. Periodically review credit limits. Ask for new credit applications from all customers annually.

Establish and Apply Collection Procedures

Your collection procedures should be firm, consistent and courteous. Think how you would like to be treated if, for reasons beyond your control, you couldn't pay a bill. Always allow your customer to save face.

Conventional business practice used to call for a series of polite letters beginning the day after an account became delinquent.

That collection procedure no longer works. The day an account becomes overdue (Day 30 if your terms are 30 days) send a reminder letter and call up the customer. Identify the person who is responsible for paying your invoice and ask politely but firmly for payment. This may take some doing particularly if you are dealing with the payables department of a large company. We have found that some of our biggest customers "lose the invoice" on a regular basis no matter what we do. Ask for reasons for non-payment if it seems necessary, but in all cases try to get a promise to pay a fixed amount on a given date. The form shown in Figure 12.6 should be filled out for every collection call. It provides hard information for future calls and also helps if you are forced into litigation.

If your polite letter and phone call do not produce almost immediate results, call again. Most people want to pay their bills—so do most businesses. By making sure that you know the person responsible for paying your account, you will move to the head of the line labeled "those to be paid." Depending on your business and depending on the importance of the customer to you, your next step will vary. The combination of letter and telephone call is difficult to top. You may wish to restrict credit until an account is made current. If so, put a note in the cus-

Figure 12.5

Credit Check

Date: _____

To: _____

Address: _____

City & State: _____

Kindly provide credit information regarding the following account:

LEDGER FACTS

Sold since: _____

To: _____

Terms: _____

Highest recent credit $ _____

Amount now owing $ _____

Amount past due $ _____

☐ satisfactory ☐ unsatisfactory

MANNER OF PAYMENT

Discounts: _____

Pays when due: _____

Days slow: _____

We will be glad to reciprocate.

Signed _____

tomer's file. You may wish to put a customer on C.O.D. terms, adding a portion of the past due debt. You may wish to set up partial payment plans, take notes or personal guarantees from the principals of the business, charge interest on the unpaid balance or use a combination of these techniques.

Some companies find night letters and mailgrams effective. It is very hard to ignore a large yellow envelope addressed to a specific individual, even in the largest corporation.

Collection agencies are a useful intermediary. They can be more aggressive. As experts who specialize in collecting debts, they can help you avoid future credit difficulties. Most reputable collection agencies use a sliding scale based on the amount of money involved and the kind of industry. 30–50 percent of the amount collected is a reasonable range. Check with your bank and trade or professional association for the best collection agency for your business.

Most importantly, do not make any threats that you do not intend to follow through on. If you say "pay within ten days or the collection agency will be after you," make sure that the collection agency will be after them.

Past due accounts present a number of problems. You don't want to offend a

---

Figure 12.6

Collections

Name: _____

Telephone: _____

Spoke To: _____

Title: _____

Subject: _____

Date: _____

Time: _____

Initials: _____

☐ No Answer   ☐ Not Available

☐ Requested Info   ☐ Requested Proof of Delivery

☐ Order Never Received   ☐ Payment Previously Sent

☐ Will Send Check   ☐ Merchandise Returned

☐ Duplicate Billing   ☐ Payment Being Held

Comments:_____

Returned Call:_____

Follow-up:_____

_____

---

good customer who is experiencing temporary difficulties. On the other hand, you don't want to subsidize someone who is sliding into bankruptcy. Know your customers as well as possible; communicate with them; and use your common sense. You will be able to help good customers while avoiding increased risks. If you suddenly begin to receive postdated or unsigned checks from a customer, or if the size of orders fluctuates greatly or unexpectedly, you may have a customer headed for trouble. Some credit experts say that you should note what bank a check is drawn on—a new bank may indicate a change in circumstances. In any case, the better you know your customer, the less likely you are to be hung up.

Monitor, Review and Change Policies as Needed

Once you have established your credit and collection policies and have put them into effect you have to monitor them. Whenever you implement a new policy you will meet with resistance.

Sometimes this resistance is appropriate. By reviewing the impact of your policies—checking to see whether or not collection periods are strictly observed and profits up—you may find that the old policies actually are the best for your business.

More likely you will find that by focusing attention on credit and collection procedures performance will improve for a time whether or not any policies are changed. You should review any changed policy after three months. You may wish to change them. You may wish to leave them in place but in any case you will be doing so for rational reasons. Ask yourself:

- Are the credit objectives we set earlier being attained?
- Has the credit capacity of the business changed?
- Should the credit policies be changed again?
- Should you aim for more average or other customers even though the bad debt risk is higher?
- Have bad debt losses and delinquency rates decreased—in dollars or in numbers?

Summary

Aim for a careful balance: Enough credit to increase sales and profitability, not too much to hurt cash flow. Careful use of credit as a sales and marketing tool will increase sales and profits. Such use is based on timely and accurate information: How good is this credit? How will it be paid—and how soon will you be repaid if the customer gets into financial trouble?

Action Steps For:
Credit and Collections

☐ Set credit objectives. What do you want your credit policies to achieve—in specific measurable terms.

☐ How much credit can your company afford to offer?

☐ Categorize customers and prospects by credit categories.

☐ Allocate credit on a customer-by-customer basis.

☐ Monitor Average collection period to measure impact of credit and collection policies.

☐ Establish and follow standard collection practices. Document all customer contacts; full notes resolve disputes in your favor.

Chapter Thirteen:

Collection Of Accounts:
A Positive Approach

Nobody enjoys pursuing deadbeats who won't pay their bills. There is no joy in seeking payment from persons who want to pay but for various reasons are unable to pay now. But these unpleasant tasks are a fact of business life. A clear credit and collection policy (see Chapter 12) will go far to minimize the need for collection practices but it won't obviate the need entirely.

Introduction

When does the average business develop procedures for the collection of accounts? Unfortunately, too often—too late. Though new firms recognize the necessity of tackling other specifics of business operations before they open their doors, the idea of problems in billing and collecting, especially delinquent accounts, is avoided like the plague. We always hope it's a predicament that will never come to pass in our business.

Thus, once the problem of a past due account finally arises with a seriousness that defies further ignoring, it is already a mess. Perhaps the customer in question has shown signs of becoming delinquent for months. Their checks have been progressively later, or smaller, with an outstanding balance looming larger, dangerously large if they are a primary customer. You, as the business owner or accounts manager have pushed the nagging worry to the back of your mind and continued to provide products or services with regular billings.

The Small Business Administration rates inability to collect monies owed as the second most common cause of new business failure, outranked only by undercapitalization.

The National Association of Credit Management has some eye-opening figures for the company who thinks they can stay on top of collections without carefully planned systems that include contingencies for slow and no payers. The Association says that as the length of time between initial billing and receipt of payment stretches on: The value of your accounts receivable dollar shrinks to 67¢ in just the first six months of delayed payment; then to an anemic 47¢ at the end of a year; and on down to a "why bother" 4¢ in five years. By the end of six months, one third of the billed dollar is gone, making the point painfully clear that prompt payment is serious business.

If you are already in business and have no established collection policy, or if your business is in the "about to be" stage, the time to set up an effective program is now, before you open those doors. If you are an established business, take this time to review your current collection policy.

Develop a Collection Policy Early

In spite of the obvious, many new business operators spend a great deal of time gaining expertise in their specialty, and no time learning to collect compensation efficiently for that specialty. Accounting procedures must be as carefully prepared as the selling of the product itself if the business is to succeed.

The main ingredients in a quality collection policy are clarity and consistency. Every new customer receives a clear contract, in simple but precise terminology, explaining the type of service they are buying, how much they will pay for that service, and the terms of payment. The contract is in writing whenever possible.

Trouble-free collection starts at the front office where sales and service personnel aim for clarity in all of their dealings with customers. A customer who buys because he has been dazzled by the verbal maneuvers of a facile sales rep may present so many problems when the reality of billing hits that the company would have been better off not to have gotten the sale at all. It's fine to use colorful methods to grab attention, but before their name goes on the dotted line that commits your company to their needs, sales pitches stop. Here contracts are produced, plain English spoken, and the nitty gritty of expectations, prices, and terms determined.

Once clarity is established and the new prospect has become a paying customer, a file is begun on their account and the next step, consistency, becomes the important factor. Every client is a favored customer. Bills, payout periods, and dates for follow-up billings and phone calls should be a consistent company policy that is the same for all. Later, when time proves that some customers are consistently good payers, meaning payment within 30 days, they will reap the benefits of your discounts for prompt payment. If your company is solid enough and cash flow strong, these customers might enjoy the extension of short-term credit. Conversely, an extremely poor payer may have to be put on a C.O.D. basis, or make deposits "up front" before their orders are filled. Again, though, these are not exceptions to your rules, but rules set up to treat exceptional cases. A collection procedure that is fair and consistent across customer lines is as necessary as quality products. These policies will save the day when overdue accounts begin to need special attention or aggressive collection.

In the interests of a uniform collection policy, specialized procedures can be set up right at the beginning which reward prompt payment and penalize dawdlers. Many new companies are unfamiliar with such techniques, even though they are common practice lately among established businesses and very easy to institute. Figure 13.1 depicts an invoice that shows a customer how much money is discounted from their bill by prompt payment. "2/10 net 30" means that a customer can take a two percent discount if payment is received within ten days, but the entire balance must be paid in 30 days. This is based on the simple idea that you, the billing company, stand to actually earn money by the interest you can generate on a positive cash flow. Margins gradually fade when funds are outstanding for as little as 10 days beyond the due date of the bill. The concept behind discounts is that savings realized by early payment are passed on to the customer at a current rate. Using the same reasoning, the billing company loses money for holding an account payable for over 30 days in most cases. Thus, a small interest charge begins to accrue against the customer's account after the 30th day. The fact that the value of accounts receivable, as we mentioned previously, begins to erode rapidly after only 30 days makes this the sensible policy. More cautious procedures with stiffer penalties in interest are usually invoked after that length of time.

Work on Potential Problems Right Away

In spite of our best efforts on behalf of impeccable billing policies, problems will develop. In the introduction, it was mentioned that the Small Business Administration identifies inability to collect monies owed as the second most prevalent cause of new business failure. The first was under-capitalization. To those of us trying to collect our bills in a timely manner, this means that too many new businesses, including a few who may become our customers, start with too little money. Because of a survival policy of waiting to get paid for deliveries to their own customers before they pay their suppliers, they often make poor payers, routinely taking 60 to 90 days or longer.

The only way to come out on top with such a company is to avoid their business when possible.

The previous chapter, Credit and Collection, focused primarily on methods for determining the credit worthiness of new customers. A thorough discussion of credit is beyond the scope of this chapter but a few key items are worth mentioning. Briefly, if you are in the position of taking on a company with no established reputation, be sure to check the company's status with its existing business colleagues, their bank's estimation of ability to pay, and most certainly, the authority of the contact person.

We have now set up collection policies, established the reputability of potential customers, and still, routine checking of invoice dates turns up an account that is 30 days from the date of original billing with no payment received. Here is where

---

Figure 13.1

INVOICE

ABC Manufacturing
1 Narrow Road
Anytown, USA

Invoice Date _____

Invoice Number _____

SOLD TO:	SHIP TO:
XYZ Distributors	XYZ Distributors
10 Broad Street	10 Broad Street
Anytown, USA	Anytown, USA

Terms: 2/10/ N 30 FBO NY	Customer Order No.		Shipped VIA		
QUANTITY		DESCRIPTION	Unit Price	Amount	TOTAL
Ordered	Shipped				
1	1	Widget	$23.50	$23.50	
3	3	Doohickies	98.95	296.85	
		Subtotal			$320.50
		Tax (where applicable) @ 4.00%			12.81
		Total Due:			333.16
		Thank you			

A 2% monthly service fee will be charged on all unpaid balances after 30 days.

---

good recordkeeping will save your billing department. Remember when the file was begun on the new account? If possible, such files should be computerized for easy storage and retrieval, making routine checks easy. Ideally, you would check the status of these files daily. If time is short— or staff at a premium, no less than once a week. On the 30th day, action commences immediately.

Due to the extent of payment problems today, and because in collection, time is money, action taken on accounts 30 days past due often starts with a phone call after an initial reminder. Ask to speak to the company officer directly responsible for accounts payable. Identify yourself and ask for that person's name. Names establish accountability. Get a firm commitment as to date, amount, and method of payment. Be polite, but steadfast, and don't allow the passage of more than 10 days before the payment of some part of the balance. Above all, always treat the party from whom you are asking payment with respect. There are specific channels of redress available if they do not act as promised. No collection problem excuses bad manners or the issuance of threats.

One successful collection agent suggests the use of sales techniques. She recommends the kind of careful listening, sincerity, and understanding of the customer's situation as expected from the sales representative when they first tried to sell the product. A top collection lawyer reflects a similar attitude in his transactions. Whenever possible, he tries to end a collection procedure on a positive note. Clarity and honesty of presentation in collection of bad debts are not only good business, they are the law. Tough consumer protection measures in most states now protect the indebted's right to be free from harassment. Follow up the phone conversation with a letter itemizing the agreement made, and put a copy, along with a notation of the phone call, in the customer's billing file. To avoid accusations of harassment, don't call or write again until the agreed upon time limit is past, then do so immediately. This kind of impeccable collecting practice will usually inspire the respect necessary to win both payment in full and continued good company relations. If it doesn't do it, stronger steps will need to be taken, but this does not change your attitude of compassion and fair dealing throughout.

The Client Who Can't Pay

You will eventually encounter the client who, for a variety of reasons not immediately resolvable, simply can't pay the bill. Assuming you have followed the recommended procedures up to now, the incidence of "can't pays" will be few and the matter can be attended to in a way that does damage to no one's business image or self-esteem beyond temporary inconvenience. From your previous attempts to collect, the basic information needed has been established and you are ready for positive action. Everyone knows whether the customer is dissatisfied, playing for time against temporary cash flow problems, or, the worst, going broke. Assuming you were clear and consistent in all prior dealings (and rapport is still good), the facts are this customer needs immediate attention. By now, no more products should be going out to this account except on a C.O.D. basis. Sometimes arrangements can be made for a portion of past due money to be added to each C.O.D. until the account is current.

In most cases, the customer will have already ceased ordering, which brings us to a variety of other workable techniques for compromise. The most obvious is an adjustment in terms. Given an extended payment period of smaller monthly installments (or weekly if prudent), the entire past due amount will likely be collectible over time. Arrange adequate interest to be included in the payments. Remember, carrying this account out over just six months will result in the loss of a third of your money if no interest is charged. A reasonable customer, and most are, will recognize your need to protect yourself from undue losses.

Installment plans and interest bring up another excellent solution: transfer of debt. Most small businesses can't afford long-term debt collection, even on behalf of a prime client, but professional lenders can. Try to transfer the debt, perhaps to a MasterCard or Visa account. The idea will be well received by the debtor who realizes that carrying the obligation out with your company will mean the higher penalty in interest that a professional lender will charge. And the extra plus is fewer inconveniences or hard feelings.

By the time everything else has been tried and the debt begins to look lost, consider cancelling full balance in favor of partial payment. Losing some is better than losing all. Partial payment compromises are underrated as acceptable last chance alternatives to litigation. Lawsuits are so costly in both money and bad company relations that the returns, usually only a portion of the debt by the time the lawyer is paid, are a Pyrrhic victory at best. However distasteful, though, legal action can become necessary in a minority of cases and must be considered as a collection final resort for the rare company who will not cooperate on another solution.

The Client Who Won't Pay

Both professional collection agents and attorneys agree that inability to pay the bills, whether it happens to a company or an individual, is unintentional and not the result of malicious intent. Therefore, the client who won't pay is usually the dissatisfied customer. Clear contracts and impeccable practices will help you ward off this kind of trouble. But suppose it happens. An unhappy client, especially one who still owes money, is a public relations problem because they feel compelled, often by guilt, to explain to your mutual business contacts why they are not paying. Compromise the difficulty, perhaps by rendering additional unbilled service, or by cancelling all or part of the balance if possible. If these solutions don't fit the magnitude of the situation, outside arbitrators can be asked by both parties to render a judgment that is binding. The Better Business Bureau runs a professional arbitration service in many towns that is free to its area businesses.

At this point in the process every conceivable avenue has been exhausted for an amicable solution, and still you feel justified in your collection attempts. Seek professional intervention, either a collection agency or an attorney, if you're sure you are in the right and the amount justifies the hassle. A reputable and effective agent or attorney may be able, by the use of the same techniques described above, combined with their professional clout, to arrange payment without going to court. Another possible alternative is small claims court, where judgments are easy to win, but hard to collect.

After having won a court judgment, you have the right to attach a debtor's assets with a lien. The problem with such drastic measures is, again, the ill will incurred, and the time it can take to collect. A debtor does not have to pay a debt secured by a lien until they wish to dispose of the encumbered assets. It could take years.

What's the Best Answer for Avoiding Collection Problems?

At a time when collection of monies owed is a growing problem, especially for the small business, the best cure is still prevention. Thus, the main focus of this article has been exactly that. Anyone can call a lawyer and go to court. The good business habits that lie at the bottom of every collection technique stressed here are those same qualities we hope for in all aspects of business and personal life. The qualities of business impeccability are: clarity in all customer dealings, both verbal and written; consistency in all company practices, with every customer; honesty; patience, when the payment can be so critical that even 10 days hurts; and compassion—put yourself in their shoes, and remember that unexpected events can cause any company to have temporary financial difficulty. No one intends to become a bad debt. The more sensitivity that can be brought to bear in collection, while still maintaining effectiveness, the better and more profitable the resolution.

Automated Accounts Receivable

Ideally, you want to know which of your customers pay on time, and who the slow-payers are. Then you can devote your attention to servicing your best customers.

A basic accounts receivable system (whether automated or not), gives you this information, especially if you age the accounts. This means listing the receivables by due dates. Normal aging is: current, 30 days, 60 days, and over 60 days.

Of the vast number of small businesses with less than $5 million dollars in sales, only about five percent have computerized accounting systems. Many businesses simply have no need for a fully-automated system, particularly if the number of customers and the amounts of receivables are small. For those businesses, a tickler file will suffice.

A basic tickler file works this way: When an invoice is sent, you enter the amount of the invoice, along with accurate customer information such as address, billing contact, etc., under the appropriate date due (30 days in most cases). At the beginning of each day, you can call up the invoices due on that particular day, and proceed from there.

Identifying what your business is and where it might be headed could be number one on the list for determining whether you need an automated system. Do you see yourself expanding in the future so that the time spent in entering figures to your ledger will become overwhelming? Also, what else would you want the system to do for your business? Are there accounting packages you need other than accounts receivable? Any system needs to be matched with what you would like it to accomplish.

Many businesses that could benefit by the use of a more sophisticated accounts receivable system are scared off by the idea of automating their accounts, either because of cost or the stories they've heard about setting up such systems.

However, there is plenty of software currently on the market emphasizing both simplicity and lower cost. Rags to Riches™, Back to Basics™, and Books ™, are only a few examples of the too-numerous-to-mention collection of software packages specially designed for small businesses.

If you are toying with the idea of automating your accounts receivable (or other accounting applications such as general ledger, accounts payable, payroll, etc.) the first logical person to check with is your accountant.

Your accountant probably uses an automated system, and can fill you in on the type of financial package in use for your particular business. He or she can help you select a program that is compatible with the methods currently in use, help you locate a dealer that sells that particular software, and may actually be interested in helping you set the system up. You are, after all, a good customer, and automating your books may make his or her work more efficient. Few computer dealers have accounting expertise.

If you feel you can't get the appropriate information from your accountant, or another CPA firm, check to see if there are any computer user groups in your area. A good example of this type of organization is The Boston Computer Society, Boston, MA, an organization aimed at furthering the public's understanding of computers. Many area groups can be a source of excellent information.

Armed with professional advice, one final suggestion is to buy locally if possible. Accounting software is well-known for demanding a bit more hand-holding at the initial start-up stage than other software packages. Having an expert available at a moment's notice can make the whole process run smooth. Proper support is the key to whether the system works, and works well.

Remember that the important idea behind purchasing the system is to make your accounting procedures easier and more accurate, so you can devote your time where it counts: tending to your most profitable customers.

Action Plan For:
Collection of Accounts

☐ Develop a collection policy based on clarity, consistency and courtesy.

☐ Set up an aging system to track all accounts, whether delinquent or not.

☐ Computerize your system; set up due dates for followup action. A tickler file is better than no system at all.

☐ Go to work on potential problems right away. Delays cost you money.

Chapter Fourteen:

Inventory Management

··

For most businesses, inventory is the largest current asset on the balance sheet. An efficient inventory management system results in greater profits—yet many businesses, old and new, pay little attention to basic inventory management tactics.

This may be due to the profound tax implications of inventory accounting. Since there have been so many accounting changes in inventory (LIFO versus FIFO, for example), we recommend that you ask your accountant how you can best take advantage of any tax breaks available.

But tax consequences, while of great importance, are secondary to the main business of turning consistent operating profits. If you manage your business with operating profits as the primary goal, then you and your accountant will be in the position to address the tax problems. If you put the tax problems first, you may lose sight of the main point: you must turn operating profits if your business is to survive and prosper.

Inventory management software has taken much of the drudgery out of the task. Consequently, such techniques as economical-ordering quantities, optimal-stocking levels, and break-even analysis will be used by more and more businesses of all sizes.

The basic ideas are straightforward: you want to buy inventory as inexpensively and economically as possible. Too little inventory results in stockouts or interruptions on the workfloor. Too much inventory results in heavier storage, handling, insurance, and financing costs, to say nothing of the increased risk of ending up with stale, outdated, or damaged goods.

How much inventory do you really need? How much can you afford? What timing should be considered? What method of monitoring inventory is appropriate for you?

These are tough questions for any business to address. But they must be answered. They can spell the difference between a profit and a loss once you add up the total cost of inventory management errors.

Review Purchasing Decisions and Procedures

Inventory management begins with careful purchasing. You can avoid most of the problems associated with inventory management if you establish clear routines to follow when ordering any new or additional inventory.

Look at how purchasing decisions are made in your business. Who makes the purchasing decisions? On what basis? The decisions must make good business sense. Any item to be put in inventory for resale, for instance, should be an item that you expect to sell in a reasonable period. Inventory turn is all-important, particularly when the carrying costs of inventory are so high.

The same management principles that govern the rest of your business apply to the purchasing process. One person has to be responsible for purchasing. Dividing this responsibility **without good business reasons** creates problems. In a large business many people may be involved with purchasing—but the same concept holds. You must be able to identify the person who makes the decisions, and that person must have the authority to match the responsibility.

Cost/price decisions must be made: Who makes them? Selecting merchandise for resale should be done within a budget: Who sets a budget—and when? Who makes the decisions?

Once these questions are settled, another set crops up—one more directly tied to the actual management of purchasing.

You need answers to the following questions:

1. Do you use purchase orders?

Even the smallest company should use standard purchase orders (POs), numbered sequentially. They help you control purchases, determine how well suppliers meet delivery

---

Figure 14.1

Inventory Carrying Costs Can Run As High As 30% When You Consider:

Insurance

Financing

Working capital

"Opportunity" costs

Taxes

Storage

Security

Handling

schedules, and provide positive evidence of what you ordered and when. POs help you time future purchases, and they provide raw data for further analysis.

2. Do you use blanket purchase agreements?

Investigate blanket purchase agreements for any item or items which you buy in large quantities. If, for example, your company buys huge amounts of sheet metal during the course of a year, your supplier might be willing to guarantee a bulk price if you contract to purchase a minimum amount during the year. You can have it delivered when you wish. If you can arrange this kind of purchase, it benefits all parties concerned. It improves your cash flow (lower costs, bills due only upon delivery of goods, predictable level of Cost of Goods Sold, no unanticipated price increases during the contract period, and so forth). Suppliers benefit because they know that your company will buy so many tons of that particular sheet metal, and they can plan accordingly.

3. Have you established economic ordering quantities?

Economic ordering quantities (EOQs) are established by studying the costs of ordering and maintaining an inventory. The major assumption here is that inventory use is uniform. If you have erratic inventories, this method may be inappropriate.

Ask your accountant to help set EOQs. Different principles apply to different businesses and your costs have to be determined—you may not have the figures readily available. However, if your inventories are used in a uniform manner over the year, and if they are substantial, EOQs can result in major savings.

Your accounting software may include an EOQ program. Since so many businesses use EOQs profitably, many electronic spreadsheets and inventory management programs incorporate EOQs as a routine offering.

4. Are stock lists available from your major suppliers?

Many distributors distill their experience in their industry into stock lists for customers. These lists can help you decide what to order, help keep you aware of what other businesses like yours are purchasing, and provide other important insights.

5. Have you set minimum and maximum stock points for specific items?

You can avoid overstocking if you set a maximum stock level on certain items. It also becomes easier to resist "bargains" on slow-moving items. It is more difficult to avoid understocking, but minimum acceptable stock levels help prevent stockouts and/or work-flow interruptions.

Figure 14.2

What Are The Important Questions When Reviewing Your Purchasing Procedures?

- Do you use purchase orders?
- Do you use blanket purchase agreements?
- Have you established EOQs?
- Are stock lists available from suppliers?
- Have you set minimum and maximum stock points for specific items?
- Do you take advantage of discounts?
- Are purchases made on a dollar available basis?
- Are purchases made only in reaction to pressing needs?
- Do you review your reorder levels at least annually?

Review both minimum and maximum points frequently—and rejustify them periodically to prevent buying out of sheer force of habit.

6. Do you take advantage of discounts?

You should. On an annualized basis, 2%/10 days, works out to 72%—a substantial amount. Ask your banker to help you work out the details. You may find that by borrowing to take advantage of discounts, you actually save cash.

7. Are purchases made on a dollar available basis?

This can be a danger sign. If your working capital is so tight that you are on a C.O.D. or cash-only basis with your suppliers, then you may have some major problems. In some cases recapitalizing the business is the only answer, but there may be other options such as securing new debt, reducing costs, or increasing productivity.

If you are put on a cash-only or C.O.D. basis by your vendors, **check into it immediately.** Was a payment inadvertently missed?

8. Are purchases made only in reaction to pressing needs?

This is another possible danger sign. Purchasing departments should anticipate needs, not react to them. While this is not always possible, there should be an earlier warning than customer complaints or stockouts to initiate the purchase of new inventory.

9. Do you review reorder levels at least annually?

Set reorder points to prevent stockouts—**and then review them.** This is one of the best ways to avoid over-stocking obsolete or slow-moving items. But don't set reorder levels and then blithely forget them. Check them—and then check the rationale behind them, one by one.

Inventory management starts with careful purchasing decisions. What—and

---

how much—do you need to have in inventory? Who makes these decisions? On what grounds? Are well-tried tools such as EOQs, reorder points, and blanket purchase agreements being used? If not, why not? Are discounts being sought? Are the basic danger signals observed?

Establish Reorder Times

Establish reorder times by looking back at sales cycles and vendor delivery times, and forward to anticipated sales and/or manufacturing forecasts.

1. Timing Based on Experience

What looks to an outsider like speculation may, for an experienced buyer, be a very carefully planned order. If you have years of experience in a particular field, then the patterns or cycles of that field become second nature.

Thoughts like "These stocks look low; next month is when the demand will boom; the supplier takes three weeks; better order tomorrow..." flash through your mind.

If you don't have the experience or if you want to make sure that others in your business understand the process, you'd go through the same steps. First, what are the stocks now? What kind of turnover do you anticipate—and do you have enough stock on hand to meet that demand? What are the reorder times? When should you place the order?

2. Reorder Points

Set reorder points on standard items—whether for resale or for assembly, for parts or office supplies. Reorder points simplify matters by doing the analysis once. It can then be applied again and again. Some consultants specialize in helping you set reorder points. Other help is available from suppliers, wholesalers and distributors, trade associations, and (in some areas) competitors.

Reorder points are great time-savers, but they do have limitations. They depend on somewhat flexible cash flow. Sales levels fluctuate, distribution patterns and suppliers may change. If your cash flow is flexible enough, you can accommodate reordering at any time and nothing interrupts the smooth flow of commerce. But you should consider these questions: What level of stockouts can you afford? How often and in what inventories?

3. Standing Orders

Standing orders with principle suppliers may be another solution. If you use blanket purchase agreements, standing orders may be appropriate. Otherwise, they suffer from the same defects as standing reorder points. They also share some of the

Figure 14.3

The Material Resource Planning (MRP) method allows you to work backwards from the time you need to have all the necessary materials delivered. Write down the length of time it takes to get each needed item (see below). If, for example, you need power cords from Taiwan and cases from West Germany, you can list the times involved and mark them on a chart as shown in Figure 14.4.

This example is taken from *How to Prosper in Your Own Business*, by Brian Smith. (Stephen Greene Press, Brattleboro, Vermont, 1981.)

Theoretical Lead Times for Ordering Materials for a Toaster

Item	Lead Time (Weeks)
Case	8
Front plate	6
Dial	1
Handle	1
Power cord	3
Harness	4
Heat coils	2
Screws	1
Legs	2
Bottom plate	3
Toast guides	5
Switch	4

The case obviously takes the longest time to receive, so it becomes the governing item from which all others are "backed off" in terms of ordering time. Figure 14.4 shows the ordering schedule for the various parts. The case is ordered on the very first day; two weeks later, the front plate is ordered; a week later than that, the toast guides are ordered, and so on.

same benefits: simple, inexpensive, and, for stable businesses, effective. But once again, tough questions come up: What inventories can you take a chance with? What level of stockouts can you afford—and in which inventories? (There are statistical techniques to help make these decisions more comfortable.) Once you are able to detect a cycle, including looking at the best and worse cases, you will ordinarily be able to set standing orders for the most stable items.

Most businesses use a combination of these three methods—because they have a mix of inventories, some of which can be managed speculatively, some on experience-based hunches, some on standard reorder points, and some on standing orders. The right mix will be a balance. If that balance has been carefully established, your chances of success are greater than if you rely on any one technique.

Check Inventories Consistently

Once you have established purchasing and timing policies for the inventories your business needs, managing the physical inventory becomes an ongoing process.

Some of the more common systems for controlling inventories are listed below, with brief explanations for each one. All are means to the same end: keeping the right inventories on hand, in the right amounts, at the right times, at the right costs.

Most businesses use a combination of these systems, since the amounts involved (and the inventory values) vary widely. Use your judgement on which ones are right for your business, and if you are not certain, call in a professional to help you make the decision.

Physical Count

Take physical counts periodically—monthly or quarterly—to make sure that balances tally with what your books say should be there. If there are serious deviations, you may have a security problem, pilferage, excessive breakage or wasting, or other problems that can easily slip by unnoticed without periodic physical counts. All other control methods are variations on this theme and must be compared at some point to an actual count.

But you don't need to take physical counts of everything at the same time. Critical inventories, or those of unusually high value, should be more carefully attended to than others. This is a matter of managerial judgement.

"Eyeball" Control

The simplest and most common method: The stock looks low, reorder. If it doesn't, let it ride.

While this is a low-cost method, it provides no systematic controls and no obvi-

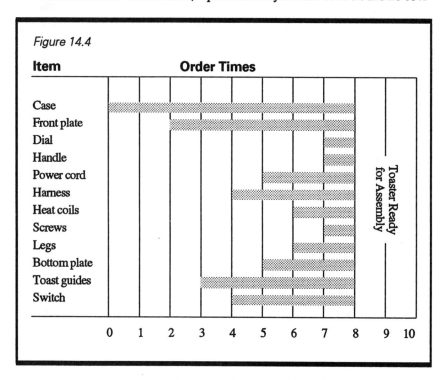

Figure 14.4

| Item | Order Times |

Figure 14.5

Your inventory turnover ratio helps you achieve a balance between over-stocking and understocking.

The formula is:

$$\frac{\text{Average Sales}}{\text{Average Inventory}} = \frac{\text{Inventory}}{\text{Turnover}}$$

Compare this ratio with industry standards and act on deviations. Too low a turnover ratio means your inventory is too large: it's not turning over fast enough. A low ratio alerts you that your inventory costs are too high and your buying practices are poor.

Too high a turnover may mean that your inventory may be too small and points to possible problems that may not be apparent otherwise: poor buying practices, illiquidity, insufficient profits, or stockouts.

Your banker or accountant will provide you with industry norms. One source is the Robert Morris Associates Annual Statement Studies. Another is your industry association and trade group publications—their editors usually have access to such information. Sometimes you can trade information with businesses similar to yours that are in different markets.

ous method of improvement (except to switch to a more formal system). Since it depends on snap evaluations, it can lead to unnecessary stockouts. For some inventories (office supplies, for example) it may be sufficient. For production or resale inventories, it's usually too simplistic.

"Brown Bag" and Bin Reserve System

If you know the acceptable minimum levels for parts and other inventories, this system works fairly well—particularly when there are large numbers of small parts that are kept in bins or on shelves.

In a brown bag or in a separate closed part of the bin or shelf, hide away the acceptable minimum. When the bin or shelf is emptied and the brown bag must be opened (or the reserve tapped), reorder.

There are many variants to this simple system, including the use of checklists and a reorder storage area (where the reserves are kept), the simpler forms of perpetual inventory systems, and periodic physical counts.

Perpetual Inventories

If you know what inventories you begin with (by actual physical count, checking against deliveries and making sure you get what you ordered), and if you know what you are using up or selling, then this kind of system makes the most sense—because as inventories are consumed, the perpetual inventory changes.

These systems can be simple: use cash register or sales slip information and lower inventories accordingly. When new shipments arrive, check the goods against the POs and shipping documentation, and increase inventory records accordingly. **Periodically, run a physical count to make sure that the perpetual inventory is accurate.**

These systems can be complex: many stores use a tag system or a bar code system to monitor inventories electronically: as a sensor is passed over the code, changes in the inventory are automatically recorded. In manufacturing plants, where there are at least three kinds of inventories (raw material, work in progress, finished goods), the systems are even more complicated and call for professional help to set up.

The great strength of perpetual inventories is the information they can provide. If you can tell, at any time, exactly what you have on hand (or should have, according to a working perpetual inventory system), purchasing and timing decisions are greatly facilitated. Slow-moving items can be isolated, and unnecessary stock levels reduced to free up working capital and make better use of floor or shelf space.

Computer Systems

Figure 14.6

Computerized Inventory Management Systems

Parts Inventory Management Module
- Materials requirements and planning report
- Parts invoice valuation
- Over/under stock
- Adjust register

Production Scheduling and Control Module
- Production work orders
- WIP-PWO sequence
- WIP-Item sequence
- Production scheduling report
- Monthly production report

Finished Goods Inventory Control Module
- Inventory valuation and gross margin report
- Adjust register
- Over/under stock
- Order desk report
- Cost of sales

Computers lend themselves to inventory management. The most obvious application is in perpetual inventory systems, but there are unlimited additional possibilities.

Some of the systems are integrated with full accounting systems; others are straightforward inventory management systems which are designed around your inventory information needs. As an indication of what you can look for, see Figure 14.6, these simple menus are just a hint at the kind of help you can get from a computerized inventory system.

However, you will still have to take occasional physical counts. There is no substitute for them. All that other systems do is provide time-saving alternatives for actual physical counts.

Review Procedures and Costs

If you lower the Cost of Goods Sold, keep carrying costs to a minimum, and prevent stockouts and interruptions due to parts or material shortage, then your inventory system will work well.

But as your company grows and processes change, you will have to review all management systems, including inventory.

Some danger signs to heed are: stockouts, customer complaints, damaged or lost goods, sudden quality control problems, lowered production, higher Cost of Goods Sold. (There are others—but these are particularly clear signals that need immediate attention.)

Careful inventory management doesn't have to be expensive or complex, but it does need to be thorough and consistent. Periodic reviews will keep your inventories under control and will increase your company's profits.

Action Plan For:
Inventory Management

☐ Review purchasing decisions and procedures: Answer the questions in Figure 14.2.

☐ Establish reorder times.

☐ Check inventories consistently.

☐ Review procedures and costs. A computerized inventory management system might pay for itself.

Chapter Fifteen:

Managing Positive Cash Flow

....

T his chapter was written by Neil Herring, a merger and acquisition specialist
with wide experience in the medical industry. Mr. Herring's advice to companies worrying about what to do with too great a cash flow is a good note to end
this book on. We should all have this problem!

Introduction

Most cash flow problems are a result of negative cash flow—a slow attrition of
the company's ability to meet current bills, panic over eroding sales, bankruptcy
or dissolution of the business if the flow isn't reversed.

But positive cash flow, desirable though it is, brings problems of its own.
Properly managed, positive cash flow allows you to increase profits, gain greater
market share, invest in other businesses, pay your employees and yourself dividends, please your bankers and investors.

Managed imprudently, positive cash flow can torpedo your business.

Approach an extended period of positive cash flow the same way you'd approach
any other business opportunity: with caution.

Determine the Source of the Positive Cash Flow

Positive cash flow—the increase in cash in your business over a period of time—can come from a number of sources. Not all of them are due to good management.

You could experience improved cash flow while going broke. Here are a few examples.

Stop paying your bills. While this might look good from a cash flow viewpoint, it will put you out of business.

Forget to pay taxes. More than one company has done this, but borrowing from Uncle Sam is expensive.

A credulous investor may have popped a substantial sum of cash into your failing enterprise.

And so on. Not all sources of positive cash flow are either beneficial or long-lasting.

The source of positive cash flow can be neutral:

You have just landed a major contract and the retainer is paid in advance.

Your business is seasonal, and this is the time of year when the money is rolling in.

Stymied by lack of capital, you have just acquired a new partner or sold some equity in your business.

You accrue funds all year to make a lump-sum payment into a pension plan and the bill is due next month.

And so on. Most of the time, positive cash flow comes from a combination of these neutral (and benign if recognized) sources, with some operating cash flow tossed in.

The best sources of positive cash flow, and the ones we all strive for, are these:

You are really making a lot of money.

Sales are up, costs are down.

Prior investments pay off.

Basically, you get positive cash flow from a very limited number of sources: new capital, new debt, sale of assets, and from operations. The first three are limited, because if the fourth doesn't chip in regularly, you run out of investors, your creditors pull the plug, and there are no assets to sell.

Hence the need to determine the sources of positive cash flow in your company.

Once you have identified the sources, your strategies for using the excess cash can be formulated—but not before. For example, if the sources are a new contract, some operating efficiencies due to investment in new equipment, plus a few deferred expenses, you might choose an aggressive strategy. However, if the sources are deferred expenses, unpaid taxes, and sale of your one money-making division, quite another strategy is called for.

Project Future Cash Flow

If you don't have a cash flow projection to guide your business, you run greater risks than you should. A cash flow budget helps you in many ways.

1. You can identify all sources of cash inflow, on a month-to-month basis. If you receive progress payments, when are they due? If your business is season-

---

Figure 15.1

A Simple Cash Flow Projection

(Note that this is for 30 days only.)
Cash on hand $1250

Line Item	Weekly	Biweekly	Monthly
Sources			
Operations:			
Accounts Rec.	$300.00	0.00	$4750.00
Cash Sales	750.00	0.00	0.00
Sale of Cash Inst.	0.00	0.00	0.00
New Debt			
New Investment			
Sale of Assets			
Uses			
Accounts Payable	$ 0.00	$600.00	$500.00
Cash Expenses	125.00	0.00	0.00
Debt Service	0.00	0.00	0.00
Payroll	0.00	1375.00	400.00
Other	200.00	200.00	200.00
Net Period Flow			
Weekly	$725.00		
Biweekly		($1450.00)	
Monthly			$600.00

The chart above indicates a typical problem with cash flow management. While there is an occasional week of substantial positive cash flow, there is also at least one week of substantial negative cash flow offsetting it. The usual strategy here would be to apply only monthly net cash flows to non-operational items. Intermonth surpluses—if any—would then be placed in a money market account or similar cash instrument.

---

al, when do you get cash? If you have a lot of receivables, when do they come due?

Since there are only four sources of cash (new debt, new investment, sale of assets, and operations), you can estimate cash inflows. List the sources of cash, breaking operating sources into Accounts Receivable, Cash Sales, Sale of Cash Instruments. Show weekly or biweekly, for a one-month period, what cash inflow you anticipate. See Figure 15.1 for an example.

2. You can identify the uses of cash on the same schedule. Don't aim for accounting perfection here. It's better to use rounded figures and get a rough idea than to bog down in precise figures. Uses of cash are pretty limited also: Accounts Payable, Cash Expenses, Debt Service, Payroll and Other (for loose ends that don't quite fit). Your bookkeeper should be able to provide these figures.

3. List major anticipated expenditures and inflows for one year. For example, if one of your customers prepays in January for the year, while one of your suppliers has to be prepaid in March for a six-month supply of raw material, you must take these cash flow oddities into account. Your aim: as few surprises as possible. You want to be able to accrue cash (or credit on a line of credit) to meet operating obligations as they fall due.

4. Subtract Outflows from Inflows on the same schedule as in 1 and 2. (Again, see Figure 15.1.)

Once you have the next month projected, apply the same steps to the next quarter and the next year. While you may have this information available now, it should be updated as your business circumstances change. If you do get a major increase in business, it will result in a major cost increase to service the sales.

Once you have a grasp of the cash flow picture for the next several months, you will understand your cash needs too. You may find, for example, that some of the idle cash can be salted away for future growth, while some will have to be available to meet next month's cash shortfall.

Figure 15.2

Sales and Expenses

Increased sales and increased expenses go together. But not in a smooth line, particularly for growing businesses. If you anticipate a substantial increase in sales over the next year, ask your accountant what this will mean in terms of:

• Operating Margins

• Fixed Costs (New plant and equipment? Increased overhead and administrative costs?)

• Profitability

Ask yourself what it will mean in terms of managerial ability and time.

Expenses (both in dollars and in management time) tend to rise in steps, not smoothly with sales. A modest increase in sales may result in greatly increased profits, because fixed expenses won't be increased. But a major sales increase can actually result in lowered profitability—and negative cash flow—if fixed expenses take an upward leap.

Establish Priorities for Your Cash Flow

Positive cash flow—from operations—creates opportunities to make more money. The way to use your cash flow will best be chosen by looking at the rate of return for each available option. Those items with the greatest potential impact on your bottom line are those which either increase revenue (without driving up fixed costs too fast) or decrease expenses (new equipment, for example).

Suppose your balance sheet looks like Figure 15.3. Reducing short-term debt of $18,500 on a line of credit would be a priority. So would increasing inventories and advertising. The question becomes: Which option makes the most sense?

You will note that the number one priority is reduction of short-term debt. Although the first two items (salaries and taxes, payables) will probably have a more dramatic effect on the company than debt reduction, keep in mind that it is easier to deposit cash against a line of credit than it is to spend it wisely. Any money not needed for immediate requirements should be used to pay down a line of credit for two significant reasons:

1. You will save substantial interest costs.

2. As a rule of thumb, your banker will be more amenable to increasing your credit line when the time comes if he can see periods when your line was only partially extended.

Research Investment Strategies and Opportunities

There are all too many ways to invest excess cash.

Some of the questions to ask yourself—once the immediate priorities have been satisfied—include:

1. Security. How safe is your money, and will it be there when you need it?

2. Liquidity. While a long-term, high rate certificate of deposit has its uses, what happens if you need the money next month, not two years from now?

3. Yield. Before investing, would the money earn more if reinvested in your company than if it were put into a cash management account? Or would a short-term investment provide the right balance of yield and liquidity for your company?

4. Time required. If your bank has a money market account, it might make more sense to use it than to seek out the best yield yourself.

Check around. If you enjoy substantial positive cash flow and want to make your cash work for you, start by asking your banker. This serves several purposes. Compensating balances may help lower your credit costs, allow you increased borrowing capacity should a need arise, and make you a more desirable bank customer.

Figure 15.3

Balance Sheet:
Your Company

December 31, 19-

Current Assets:

Cash	$ 1,250
Accounts Rec.	6,725
Deposits	1,420
Inventory	18,300
Subtotal:	$27,695

Fixed Assets:

Furniture & Equipment	$ 3,100
Capitalized Leases	5,695
Startup Costs	1,780
Less accum. dep.	(4,310)
Subtotal:	$ 6,265
TOTAL ASSETS:	$ 33,960

Current Liabilities:

Trade Payables	$1,830
Accrued Salaries & Taxes	2,700
Current Por. Cap. Leases	1,300
Demand Note Payable	18,500
Subtotal:	$24,330

Long-Term Debt

Capitalized Lease Oblig.	$ 2,295
Subtotal:	$ 2,295

Owner's Equity

100 Shares Common Stock	$1,000
Paid in Capital	19,000
Retained Earnings (Loss)	(15,765)
Fiscal Year Net Profit	3,100
Subtotal:	$ 7,335

Total Liabilities & Equity: $ 33,960

Keep your aims clear, however. You want safety and liquidity first, then yield. This doesn't mean to let excess cash idle, just that your business should make its profits on operations, not on investments.

Choose the Appropriate Strategy and Stick to It

Based on your analysis of your business' needs and opportunities, you can now begin to maximize the return on your excess cash. Be consistent and be sure that your strategies are part of the long-term business plan.

For example, suppose that you have asked your bank to set up a sweep account to be used whenever balances rise above a preset limit This allows current obligations to be funded, yet makes sure that idle funds will do some work for you. The excess cash will be swept daily into a high-interest money market account, immediately available if needed for operational purposes.

By keeping borrowing low, you reduce interest costs. In most cases, interest you pay is higher than interest you would receive from an investment. On the other hand, there can be good reasons to keep cash liquid rather than paying down a line of credit or reducing other debt.

For example, you may be approaching year-end, and you want to be able to use your financial statements for raising more debt or new equity investment. A strong acid test ratio (cash and near cash divided by current liabilities) can make investors drool—and with a positive cash flow, handling long-term debt would not be a problem. "Prettying up" your balance sheet can pay off, whether you are a multinational company, a corner store, or somewhere in between.

The important thing is that you adopt your cash flow strategy to your business plan. If you know what cash you will need, when you will need it, and why, you can make consistently fine decisions.

Once you adopt a strategy, stick to it until conditions change. Note the "until conditions change." No strategy is good forever, and no strategy works if it isn't implemented.

Figure 15.4

Cash Flow Priorities: Your Company

Description	Amount	Notes
1. Reduce credit line	_____	_____
	_____	_____
	_____	_____
2. Increase inventory	_____	_____
	_____	_____
	_____	_____
3. Increase advertising	_____	_____
	_____	_____
	_____	_____

Note that the priority list refers to your business plan, your cash budget and the credit line limit of $30,000. These notes can spell the difference between dreaming and achievement.

Action Plan For:
Managing Positive Cash Flow

☐ Determine the source of the positive cash flow. Is it from operations? Or from less desirable sources?

☐ Project future cash flow, weekly, monthly, yearly.

☐ Establish priorities for investing excess cash flow. Check it against your business plan.

☐ Research investment strategies and opportunities.

☐ Choose the appropriate strategy and stick to it.

Resources for Small Businesses

··

There are many excellent texts available on small business management, but most are more appropriate for businesses with more than 100 employees. Check out your local library, college bookstores and these sources of small business management information:

Upstart Publishing Company, Inc. These publications on proven management techniques for small businesses are available from Upstart Publishing Company, Inc., 12 Portland Street, Dover, NH 03820. For a free current catalog, call 800-235-8866 outside New Hampshire, or 749-5071 in state.

- *The Business Planning Guide*, 1992, David H. Bangs, Jr. and Upstart Publishing Company, Inc. A manual that helps you write a business plan and financing proposal tailored to your business, your goals and your resources. Includes worksheets and checklists. (Softcover, 208 pages, $19.95)

- *The Market Planning Guide*, 1990, David H. Bangs, Jr. and Upstart Publishing Company, Inc. A manual to help small-business owners put together a goal-oriented, resource-based marketing plan with action steps, benchmarks and timelines. Includes worksheets and checklists to make implementation and review easier. (Softcover, 160 pages, $19.95)

- *The Cash Flow Control Guide*, 1990, David H. Bangs, Jr. and Upstart Publishing Company, Inc. A manual to help small-business owners solve their number-one financial problem. Includes worksheets and checklists. (Softcover, 88 pages, $14.95)

- *The Personnel Planning Guide*, 1988, David H. Bangs, Jr. and Upstart Publishing Company, Inc. A 176-page manual outlining practical, proven personnel management techniques, including hiring, managing, evaluating and compensating personnel. Includes worksheets and checklists. (Softcover, 176 pages, $19.95)

- *The Start Up Guide: A One-Year Plan for Entrepreneurs*, 1989, David H. Bangs, Jr. and Upstart Publishing Company, Inc. This book utilizes the same step-by-step, no-jargon method as the *Business Planning Guide*, to help even those with no business training through the process of beginning a successful business. (Softcover, 160 pages, $19.95)

- *Managing by the Numbers: Financial Essentials for the Growing Business*, 1992, David H. Bangs, Jr. and Upstart Publishing Company, Inc. Straightforward techniques for getting the maximum return with a minimum of detail in your business' financial management. (Softcover, 160 pages, $19.95)

- *On Your Own: A Woman's Guide to Building a Business*, 1990, Laurie Zuckerman, Upstart Publishing Company, Inc. *On Your Own* is for women who want hands-on, practical information about starting and running a business. It deals honestly with issues like finding time for your business when you're also the primary care provider, societal biases against women and credit discrimination. (Softcover, 224 pages, $18.95)

- *Buy the Right Business—At the Right Price*, 1990, Brian Knight and the Associates of Country Business, Inc., Upstart Publishing Company, Inc. Many people who would like to be in business for themselves think strictly of starting a business. In some cases, buying a going concern may be preferable—and just as affordable. (Softcover, 152 pages, $18.95)

- *Borrowing for Your Business*, 1991, George M. Dawson, Upstart Publishing Company, Inc. This is a book for borrowers and about lenders. Includes detailed guidelines on selecting a bank and a banker, answering the lender's seven most important questions, how your banker looks at a loan and how to get a loan renewed. (Hardcover, 160 pages, $19.95)

- *Problem Employees*, 1991, Dr. Peter Wylie and Dr. Mardy Grothe, Upstart Publishing Company, Inc. Provides managers and supervisors with a simple, practical and straightforward approach to help all employees, especially problem employees, significantly improve their work performance. (Softcover, 272 pages, $22.95)

- *Marketing Sourcebook for Small Business*, 1989, Jeffrey P. Davidson, John Wylie Publishing. A good introductory book for small business owners with excellent definitions of important marketing terms and concepts. (Hardcover, 325 pages, $24.95)

- *Guerilla Marketing: Secrets for Making Big Profits from Your Small Business,* 1984, J. Conrad Levinson, Houghton-Mifflin. A classic tool kit for small businesses. (Hardcover, 226 pages, $14.95)

- *Forecasting Sales and Planning Profits: A No Nonsense Guide for a Growing Business,* 1986, Kenneth E. Marino, Probus Publishing Co., Concise and easily applied forecasting system based on an analyses of market potential and sale requirements which helps establish the basis for financial statements in your business plan. (Hardcover, 177 pages)

Periodicals

Small Business Reporter. An excellent series of booklets on small business management published by Bank of America, Department 3120, PO Box 37000, San Francisco, CA 94137 (415) 622-2491. Individual copies are $5 each. Ask for a list of current titles—they have about 17 available, including *Steps to Starting a Business, Avoiding Management Pitfalls, Business Financing* and *Marketing Small Business.*

In Business. A bimonthly magazine for small businesses, especially those with less than 10 employees. The publisher is J.G. Press, PO Box 323, Emmaus, PA 18049. Annual Subscriptions are $18.

Inc. magazine. One of the leading small business magazines. 38 Commercial Wharf, Boston, MA 02110 (617) 248-8000.

D & B Reports. Excellent case studies and updated financial information for small businesses. Dun and Bradstreet, 299 Park Ave., New York, NY 10171 (212) 593-6724.

Small Business Forum: Journal of the Association of Small Business Development Centers. Case studies and analyses of small business problems gleaned from a nationwide network of small business development professionals. Includes book reviews. Reprints available. Issued three times a year, $25.00 per year. University of Wisconsin, SBDC, 432 North Wake St., Madison, WI 53706.

Other Tools for Small Business Owners

Software for small businesses. We recommend fisCAL™, a product of the Halcyon Group, 449 Fleming Rd., Charleston, SC 29412 (803) 795-7336. fisCAL™ and its accompanying manual, *Profit from Financial Statements*, provides a sophisticated financial analysis system for most small businesses. fisCAL™ includes updated financial data from the Robert Morris Associates (RMA) Annual Statement Studies, financial research associates, Financial Statement Studies of the Small Business Annual and Halcyon's Financial Profiles of the Small Business.

Financial Templates. PSI Research 300 N. Valley Drive, Grants Pass, OR 97526 offers excellent financial templates for small-business owners. Small Business Expert is for use with IBM and compatibles and Financial Templates for Small Business is for use with Excel™ on the Macintosh™. You may also find ready-made templates for specific business applications available from local computer clubs.

Additional
Resources

··

Small Business Development Centers (SBDCs). Call your state university or the Small Business Administration (SBA) to find the SBDC nearest you. Far and away the best free management program available, SBDCs provide expert assistance and training in every aspect of business management. Don't ignore this resource.

SCORE, or Service Corps of Retired Executives, sponsored by the U.S. Small Business Administration, provides free counseling and also a series of workshops and seminars for small businesses. Of special interest: SCORE offers a Business Planning Workshop which includes a 30-minute video produces specifically for SCORE by Upstart Publishing and funded by Paychex, Inc. There are over 500 SCORE chapters nationwide. For more information, contact the SBA office nearest you and ask about SCORE.

Small Business Administration (SBA). The SBA offers a number of management assistance programs. If you are assigned a capable Management Assistance Officer, you have an excellent resource. The SBA is worth a visit, if only to leaf through their extensive literature.

Colleges and universities. Most have business courses. Some have SBDCs, others have more specialized programs. Some have small-business expertise—the University of New Hampshire, for example, has two schools which provide direct small-business management assistance.

Keye Productivity Center, P.O. Box 23192, Kansas City, MO 64141. Keye Productivity offers business seminars on specific personnel topics for a reasonable fee. Call them at 800-821-3919 for topics and prices. Their seminar entitled Hiring and Firing is excellent, well-documented and useful. Good handout materials are included.

Comprehensive Accounting Corporation, 2111 Comprehensive Drive, Aurora, IL 60507. CAC has over 425 franchised offices providing accounting, bookkeeping and management consulting services to small businesses. For information, call 800-323-9009.

Center for Entrepreneurial Management, 29 Greene Street, New York, NY 10013. The oldest and largest nonprofit membership association for small-business owners in the world. They maintain an extensive list of books, videotapes, cassettes and other small-business management aids. Call 212-925-7304 for information.

Libraries. Do not forget to take advantage of the information readily available at your library.

Index